I0804798

Staffordshire Figures
1780–1840
Volume 4

Myrna Schkolne

Schiffer Publishing Ltd

4880 Lower Valley Road • Atglen, PA 19310

Copyright © 2014 by Myrna Schkolne

Library of Congress Control Number: 2013944801

All rights reserved. No part of this work may be reproduced or used in any form or by any means—graphic, electronic, or mechanical, including photocopying or information storage and retrieval systems—without written permission from the publisher.

The scanning, uploading, and distribution of this book or any part thereof via the Internet or via any other means without the permission of the publisher is illegal and punishable by law. Please purchase only authorized editions and do not participate in or encourage the electronic piracy of copyrighted materials.
"Schiffer," "Schiffer Publishing, Ltd. & Design," and the "Design of pen and inkwell" are registered trademarks of Schiffer Publishing, Ltd.

Cover designed by: Bruce Waters
Type set in Bernhard Modern BT/Arrus BT

ISBN: 978-0-7643-4540-1
Printed in China

Published by Schiffer Publishing, Ltd.
4880 Lower Valley Road
Atglen, PA 19310
Phone: (610) 593-1777; Fax: (610) 593-2002
E-mail: Info@schifferbooks.com

For our complete selection of fine books on this and related subjects, please visit our website at www.schifferbooks.com. You may also write for a free catalog.

This book may be purchased from the publisher. Please try your bookstore first.

We are always looking for people to write books on new and related subjects. If you have an idea for a book, please contact us at proposals@schifferbooks.com.

Schiffer Publishing's titles are available at special discounts for bulk purchases for sales promotions or premiums. Special editions, including personalized covers, corporate imprints, and excerpts can be created in large quantities for special needs. For more information, contact the publisher.

Contents

About Values and Titles

Values

This work uses the following scale as an approximation of value.

Price A: Up to $1,000 (£625)
Price B: $1,001–$3,000 (£626–£1,875)
Price C: $3,001–$6,000 (£1,876–£3,750)
Price D: $6,001–$9,000 (£3,751–£5,626)
Price E: $9,001–$15,000 (£5,626–£9,375)
Price F: $15,001–$25,000 (£9,376–£15,625
Price G: $25,001 and over (£15,626 and above)

The value of a figure is a function of the standard of its modeling and decoration, its condition, its scarcity, and the appeal of the subject. Essentially, value is quirky, and it can be somewhat subjective. Many small figures are highly desirable and difficult to procure, yet they fall into Price A—even though collectors value them more highly than mediocre figures in higher price brackets.

The determinants of value are not apparent from a photograph, and seemingly identical figures may have vastly different values. The values indicated in captions are not auction values or resale values. Rather, they are the values of figures purchased from a reputable retail source. In each case, the value is an estimate of the value of the figure illustrated. A very similar figure may be worth significantly more or less, depending on the condition and the quality of the glazes and enamels. At the same time, condition issues are not always apparent in a photograph, and, out of respect for those supplying photographs of their treasures for this work, condition reports have not been attached to captions. For that reason, condition is only factored into the value equation to the extent that issues are apparent in the photograph or are known to the author.

Titles

Please note that figure titles are frequently misspelled and have been reproduced in the captions as they appear on the figures.

Family, Friendship, and Play

138. Courtship

Courtship groups portray courtship in an era when romantic rituals were vastly different from those of today. In the much-loved "Sherratt" interpretation, the courting couple appears older and the gentleman offers a ring (figs. 138.1–3). This group is usually on a low mound base, and it has been noted with the bocage arranged in an arc. The Earle Collection (no. 645) shows a titled example on a table base with the couple flanked by pillars that once supported an arch. Similar pillars with arches are found on "Sherratt" figures of Elijah, the Widow, Neptune, Venus, and the Reading Maid.

The group known as Perswaition features a youthful courting couple, and again the gentleman offers a ring (figs. 138.5–9). In rare instances, *PERSWAITION* is impressed on a small tablet on the base. The figure group's design source is a print titled *Persuasion* published in 1809. All examples are attributed to the Patriotic Group.

In the courtship scenes in figures 138.10–14, the courting couple sits on a mound base rather than a bench, and there is no indication of a ring. "Sherratt" and John Dale made such groups titled *COURT SHIP* and *COURTSHIP* respectively, so there is little doubt that they do indeed portray a courting scene.

Figure 138.1. *COURT SHIP*. Gentleman offers a ring to his lady; with bocage. Attributed to "Sherratt". H: 7.9". This attractive group is not often titled. The base and the combination of bocage leaves and flowers are specific to "Sherratt". Price D. *Brighton and Hove Museums*.

Figure 138.2. *COURT SHIP*. Gentleman offers a ring to his lady; with bocage. Attributed to "Sherratt". H: 7.6". Like the preceding example but on a less common "Sherratt" base. Price D.

Figure 138.3. Courtship. Gentleman offers a ring to his lady; with bocage. Attributed to "Sherratt". H: 7.5". Like the preceding examples but on a typical "Sherratt" feathered base. Price D.

Figure 138.4. *Persuasion*, published by W. D. Walker, 1809. Reverse-painted print applied to glass. This image, rather than Jane Austen's *Persuasion* (published in 1818), inspired earthenware "Perswaition" groups. Note that the figures in the groups are reversed.

Figure 138.5. *PERSWAITION*. The gentleman offers a ring to his lady; with bocage. Attributed to Patriotic Group. H: 7". This group is rarely titled. Price D. © *Victoria and Albert Museum, London*.

Figure 138.6. Perswaition. The gentleman offers a ring to his lady; with bocage. Attributed to Patriotic Group. H: 8.1". This pinecone bocage is specific to Patriotic Group. Price D.

Figure 138.7. Perswaition. The gentleman offers a ring to his lady; with bocage. Attributed to Patriotic Group. H: 8". Like previous and following examples but with a different bocage, the flowers on it being exclusive to the Patriotic Group. Price C. *Whitehall Antiques, Chapel Hill, North Carolina*.

Figure 138.8. Perswaition. The gentleman offers a ring to his lady; with bocage. Attributed to Patriotic Group. H: 8.7". The bocage fronds each have three hawthorn leaves, and the base is typical of the Group. Price C.

Figure 138.9. Perswaition. The gentleman offers a ring to his lady; with bocage. Attributed to Patriotic Group. H: 8.7". An uncommon variant on luster feet with a bocage of hawthorn fronds. Price D.

Figure 138.10. *COURTSHIP*. The gentleman embraces his lady; with bocage. Impressed "I. DALE BURSLEM". H: 7.6". The only marked example known. Restored bocage. Price B.

Figure 138.11. *COURT SHIP*. The gentleman embraces his lady; with bocage. Attributed to "Sherratt". H: ~9". The figures are similar to those in the Dale courtship group previously shown. The only recorded "Sherratt" example. Companion to figure 148.7. Restored bocage. Price B.

Figure 138.12. Courtship. The gentleman embraces his lady; with bocage. Possibly by "Sherratt". H: ~7.6". "Sherratt" used this bocage (five-leaflet fern fronds). Companion to figure 148.8. Price B.

Figure 138.13. Courtship. The gentleman embraces his lady; with bocage. Price B. *John Howard; www.antiquepottery.co.uk.*

Figure 138.14. Courtship. The gentleman embraces his lady; with bocage. Attributed to Tunstall Group. H: ~7.5". The bocage flowers are characteristic of "Tunstall". Bocages painted similarly occur on other Tunstall examples. Companion to figure 148.14. Price B.

Figure 138.15. Courtship. The gentleman stands with his arm around the lady; with bocage. Probably attributable to Straw Flower Group. H: ~6". A rare group, known from only this example. The tiny bocage flowers (each with five cleft petals) and other subtle nuances suggest the attribution. Price B.

Figure 138.16. Courtship. The gentleman offers garlands to his lady; with bocage. H: 7.5". Price B. *The William Herbert and Nancy Hunt Collection.*

Figure 138.17. Details of the bocage and flower basket on the previous example. This bocage is only otherwise documented on small Dr. Syntax groups. *The William Herbert and Nancy Hunt Collection.*

Figure 138.18. Kissing couple, her shoe dropped in her throes of passion; with bocage. H: 4.7". Price A.

Figure 138.19. Kissing couple, her shoe dropped in her throes of passion or lust. H: ~4.7". Made without bocage. Price A.

Figure 138.20. Kissing children, he unclad. H: 3.4". The back is flat and unpainted. Note the gilding on her hair band. The same motif (probably from the same mold) appears on the sides of a dovecote (Vol. 3, figs. 113.1–2). Price B.

139. Weddings

Staffordshire wedding groups most commonly portray one of two marriage scenes. In anvil wedding groups, the wedding takes place at the blacksmith's anvil in Gretna Green, with the blacksmith officiating. In New Marriage Act groups, a cleric officiates, and a plaque commemorates the passage of the New Marriage Act.

Figure 139.1. Gretna Green marriage group (L) and the New Marriage Act group (R); with bocage. H: 7.4". An original pairing. Price E.

Figure 139.2. Detail of the plaques on the Gretna Green and New Marriage Act groups figure 139.1.

The blacksmith's shop in Gretna Green, Scotland, was the venue of choice for runaway brides and grooms, so marriage groups depicting a blacksmith marrying a couple are called Gretna Green weddings (figs. 139.1–15). Sometimes they are dubbed "anvil weddings" because the wedding party stands at the anvil. Their design source is a print titled *Gretna Green, or the Red-Hot Marriage*, circa 1795.

In the early 1800s, England had very rigorous marriage laws. A couple not wanting to comply could go to Scotland where, providing they had reached sixteen years of age, they could plight their troth in the presence of any two witnesses and be married. The first village across the Scottish border on a major roadway was Gretna Green—and the blacksmith's shop on the outskirts of the village was a convenient stopping point for couples fleeing family intent on stopping their union. The romantic notion was that the blacksmith, who forged hot metal at the anvil, forged binding unions.

Some anvil wedding groups have plaques reading "JOHN MACDONALD AGED 79 A SCOTCH ESQUIRE RUN OF WITH A ENGLISH GIRL AGED 17 TO GRATNAL GREEN THE OLD BLACKSMITH TO BE MARRIED". It is suggested that such groups poked fun at the aged Lord Erskine, who, in October 1818, ran off to Gretna Green with his young housekeeper, Sarah Buck, and their three illegitimate children. Lord Erskine supposedly traveled disguised as a lady to elude his legitimate children who opposed the marriage.

Gretna Green wedding groups are more difficult to procure than New Marriage Act groups. The "Sherratt" model is larger and never has a plaque, but most others do. However, some examples have lost the plaque and some were made without a plaque. Only one Gretna Green group within an arbor has been recorded.[1]

Figure 139.3. *Gretna Green, or the Red-Hot Marriage*, published circa 1795.

Figure 139.4. *WEDDING*. Gretna Green wedding. The blacksmith is marrying the bride and groom; with dog, with spill vase and bocage. Attributed to "Sherratt". L: 9.5". The base, the turrets, and the bocage are distinctively "Sherratt". This group is longer than similar "Sherratt" groups on footed bases. Price D.

Figure 139.5. Gretna Green wedding. The blacksmith is marrying the bride and groom; with spill vase and bocage. Attributed to "Sherratt". H: 8.1". On a characteristic feathered base. Restored figures, dog missing. Price B.

Figure 139.6. *WEDDING, WEDDING*. Gretna Green wedding. The blacksmith is marrying the bride and groom; with dog, spill vase and bocage. Attributed to "Sherratt". H: 8.5". This fern leaf bocage with mayflowers is characteristic of "Sherratt," as is the base. Price D. *Collection of Michael J. Smith*.

Figure 139.7. Gretna Green wedding. The blacksmith is marrying the bride and groom; with dog, spill vase and bocage. Attributed to "Sherratt". H: 8". On a typical "Sherratt" brown table base. Price D. *Jonathan Horne.*

Figure 139.8. *WEDDING*. Gretna Green wedding. The blacksmith is marrying the bride and groom; with dog, spill vase, and bocage. Attributed to "Sherratt". H: 9". An unusual variation known from only this example. Price C. *The William Herbert and Nancy Hunt Collection.*

Figure 139.9. Gretna Green wedding. The blacksmith is marrying the bride and groom; with bocage. H: 7.5". On a distinctive, brightly painted base. Price C.

Figure 139.10. Gretna Green wedding. The blacksmith is marrying the bride and groom; with bocage. H: ~7.5". Made without a plaque. Companion to a New Marriage Act (fig. 139.26). Price B. *Michael Goodacre.*

Figure 139.11. Gretna Green wedding. The blacksmith is marrying the bride and groom; with bocage. Attributed to Patriotic Group. H: ~8". The holly bocage is specific to the Group. Companion to a New Marriage Act (fig. 139.28). Price C. *Andrew Dando Antiques.*

Figure 139.12. Gretna Green wedding, reverse of previous group. *Andrew Dando Antiques.*

Figure 139.13. Gretna Green wedding. The blacksmith is marrying the bride and groom; with bocage. Attributed to Patriotic Group. H: ~8". The holly bocage is characteristic of the Group, but its berries are normally painted red or pink. Price B.

Figure 139.14. Gretna Green wedding. The blacksmith is marrying the bride and groom; with bocage. H: 7.9". Similar colorful bases also occurs on figures of Jobson and Nell (Vol. 2, fig. 44.14) and on a New Marriage Act group (fig. 139.27). Price B. *Brighton and Hove Museums.*

Figure 139.15. Gretna Green wedding. The blacksmith is marrying the bride and groom; with bocage. H: ~8". The base is similar to that of the preceding example, but the bocage (anthemion leaves) differs. Both may be from the same pot bank. Companion to figure 139.27. Price B.

Figure 139.16. Blacksmith performing the marriage ceremony at the anvil; with bocage. H: ~6". Probably other figures in conjunction with this portrayed a Gretna Green vignette. Price B.

Figure 139.17. Bride and groom, he offers a ring; with bocage. H: 5.1". The figures of the bride and groom are the same models used in Gretna Green wedding groups. White wedding dresses were not yet customary, so brides in all the groups wear colorful garb. Price B.

In New Marriage Act figure groups, the bride and groom stand before a parson, while a young clerk comically beseeches the heavens for approval of the union (figs. 139.18–33). These groups commemorate the passage of The New Marriage Act of 1823, legislation that reinforced marriage. Prior to 1823, persnickety marriage law requirements made marriage difficult, and they also made it quite easy to make a mistake. If a couple failed to comply with all the rules, their marriage was not legal and either party could seek an annulment, even many years later. Even if both parties were quite happy to end their marriage, an annulment had disastrous financial consequences for children who unexpectedly found themselves declared illegitimate. Society expected marriage to last for life, so the Marriage Act of 1823 made it no longer possible to annul a marriage because of a petty violation of the marriage law.

Most New Marriage Act groups include a plaque reading "THE NEW MARRIAGE ACT. JOHN FRILL AND ANN BOKE AGED 21 THAT IS RIGHT SAYS THE PARSON AMEN SAYS THE CLARK". In other words, whatever the true age of either John or Ann, who claimed to be twenty-one years old and thus of marrying age, they were married. Amen. There was no going back!

Figure 139.18. New Marriage Act. The bride and groom stand with the parson and clerk; with bocage. H: 7.5". A rarer group than the following examples on square bases, and the figures are significantly larger. Note the anthemion bocage leaves and the flowers on the branches, rather than on the leaves. Price C.

Figure 139.19. New Marriage Act, detail of the previous example. The faces are very expressive, and her finger sticks out, ready for a ring.

Figure 139.20. New Marriage Act. The bride and groom stand with the parson and clerk; with bocage. H: ~7". Price C. *John Howard; www.antiquepottery.co.uk.*

Figure 139.21. New Marriage Act. The bride and groom stand with the parson and clerk; with bocage. H: 6.5". Price C. © *Victoria and Albert Museum, London*

Figure 139.22. New Marriage Act. The bride and groom stand with the parson and clerk; with bocage. Possibly attributable to Blue Group. H: 6.8". Price C. *Collection of Susan and Richard Cann.*

Figure 139.23. New Marriage Act, reverse of previous example. The flower stalks, used to attach flowers to the bocage, are painted to simulate flowers. *Collection of Susan and Richard Cann.*

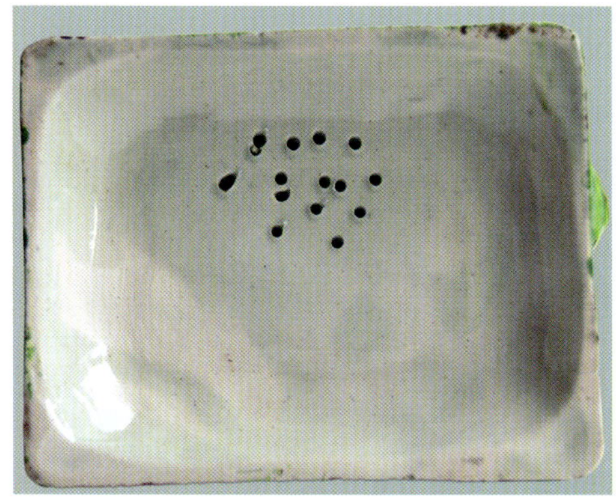

Figure 139.24. Base of previous New Marriage Act. Multiple small vent holes are punched into the base. *Collection of Susan and Richard Cann.*

Figure 139.25. New Marriage Act. The bride and groom stand with the parson and clerk; with bocage. Attributed to Leaf Mat Group. H: 6.9". On the plaque, "clerk" is spelled "CLAERK". Price B. *Brunk Auctions, Asheville, North Carolina.*

Figure 139.26. New Marriage Act. The bride and groom stand with the parson and clerk; with bocage. H: ~7". Companion to a Gretna Green group (fig. 139.10). Made without a plaque. Price B.

Figure 139.27. New Marriage Act. The bride and groom stand with the parson and clerk; with bocage. H: ~7". A companion Gretna Green group is in figure 139.15. Price B.

Figure 139.28. New Marriage Act. The bride and groom stand with the parson and clerk; with bocage. Attributed to Patriotic Group. H: 7.4". Has a characteristic holly bocage. Companion to figure 139.11. "Marriage" is impressed as "MARREG". Price B. *Stair Galleries*.

Figure 139.29. New Marriage Act. The bride and groom stand with the parson and clerk; with bocage. Attributed to Patriotic Group. H: ~7.2". Like the preceding example. Bases painted in this manner occur on other examples from this pot bank. "Marriage" is again impressed "MARREG". Price B.

Figure 139.30. New Marriage Act. The bride and groom stand with the parson and clerk; with bocage. Attributed to Patriotic Group. H: 7.2". Like the preceding two examples but with a different bocage consistent with attribution. Again, "marriage" is impressed "MARREG". Price B.

Figure 139.31. New Marriage Act. The bride and groom stand with the parson and clerk; with bocage. Attributed to Blue Group. H: ~7". The bocage is characteristic of the Blue Group. Price B.

Figure 139.32. New Marriage Act. The bride, groom, parson, and clerk stand in an arbor. H: 6.1". Arbor groups vary slightly in the placement of the figures and plaque and the decoration of the arbor. This group was reproduced into the twentieth century. Price C.

Figure 139.33. New Marriage Act. The bride, groom, parson, and clerk stand in an arbor. H: ~6". Price C.

140. Who Shall Ware the Breches

The contest for the breeches is a theme that has aroused mirth for centuries, and medieval carvings and illustrations testify to the significance of this age-old struggle. In the early 1800s, matrimonial battles raged unabated because there was no divorce law. Marriage vows did not ensure eternal bliss, and the battle for the breeches captured in Staffordshire clay symbolizes the inescapable matrimonial turmoil of bygone times. Usually carrying the amusing and typically misspelled inscriptions *Who Shall Ware the Breches* and *Conquer or Die*, these figure groups are pointed reminders that death generally provided the only release from a miserable marriage.

Who Shall Ware the Breches groups are particularly rare and desirable. Two variations occur. One is on a claw-footed table base and has a rounded top. The other is on a rectangular slab base, has a pointed top, and a baby bundled in blankets is on the base. Nine examples are on record.[1] Some attribute these groups to "Sherratt," but there is no basis for that attribution.

Figure 140.1. *WHO SHALL WARE THE BRECHES, CONQUER OR DIE*. Man and lady battling over breeches, with spill vase. H: 8.1". The arms and breeches in these groups are vulnerable to damage. Here all are original. Note the man's raised clenched fist. Price E.

Figure 140.2. *WHO SHALL WARE THE BRECHES, CONQUER OR DIE*. Previous example showing the open spill vase. The words *CONQUER OR DIE* are well impressed but have not been painted.

Figure 140.3. *WHO SHALL WARE THE BRECHES, CONQUER OR DIE*. Man and lady battling over breeches, with spill vase. H: 8.2". Price E. *Collection of Arnold and Barbara Berlin*.

Figure 140.4. *CONQUER OR DIE, WHO SHALL WEAR THE TROUSERS*. Man and lady battling over breeches; with spill vase. H: 7.5". The only example with "wear" spelled correctly and TROUSERS rather than BRECHES. The baby on the base only occurs on examples on flat bases. Price E. *Brighton and Hove Museums*.

Figure 140.5. *CONQUER OR DIE, WHO SHALL WARE THE BRECHES*. Man and lady battling over breeches; with spill vase. H: 7.3". The bundled baby on the floor may be modeled or place differently from that in the figure 140.4. Price E. © *Victoria and Albert Museum, London*.

141. Old Age

Old age is depicted in figural form as an elderly gentleman and lady. Several pot banks made such figures, suggesting that this was a popular theme in its time. The figures are, in most cases, stylistically similar and probably have a common pictorial design source. To modern eyes, they are rather grim portrayals of old age, but in the early nineteenth century, premature death and disability were commonplace, and reaching old age was an achievement to be celebrated.

Figure 141.1. Old Age. An aged couple; with bocage. H: 10.5". The only known example of this couple as a group. From the same pot bank as Vol. 2, fig. 96.13 (Lost Coin and Lost Sheep together on this base and with this bocage). Price B.

Figure 141.2. Old Age. An old lady; with bocage. H: ~8.4". Probably from the same pot bank as the following two figures. The back of the bocage is unpainted. Price A.

Figure 141.3. Old Age. An old lady; with bocage. H: ~8.4". Similar to the preceding figure but with different bocage leaves. Made with bocage on one side only. Price A.

Figure 141.4. Old Age. An old lady. H: ~8.4". Like the preceding two figures but made without a bocage. The same cluster of flowers is on the base of this and the previous figure. Price A.

Figure 141.5. Old Age. An old gentleman; with bocage. H. 8.2". Made with bocage on one side only. The cluster of flowers on the bases of the previous two figures occurs on this bocage, and the three figures are probably all from the same pot bank. Price A. *Brighton and Hove Museums*.

Figure 141.6. *Old Age*. An old lady; with bocage. Attributed to Ralph Wood. H. 9.9". The bocage, titling, and the decoration of the base support the attribution. The interior of the base is atypical in that it is sharply squared, not having the rounded corners usually on Ralph Wood bases. Price A.

Figure 141.7. *Old Age*, reverse of previous figure.

Figure 141.8. *Old Age*. An old gentleman. Attributed to Ralph Wood. H. 8.3". Companion subject to figure 141.7 but made without bocage. Price A. *Nick Burton*.

Figure 141.9. *Old Age*, reverse of previous figure. *Nick Burton*.

Figure 141.10. *OLD AGE, OLD AGE*. An old gentleman and an old lady, a pair. H: 7". Made without bocages. Price B. *Collection of Michael J. Smith.*

Figure 141.11. *OLD AGE*. An old gentleman. H: 6.9". Probably from the same unidentified pot bank as the previous old man, but here the scrolls on the base are painted blue. Made without bocage. Price A. *Elinor Penna.*

Figure 141.12. *OLD AGE*. An old lady. H: 6.9". Probably from the same pot bank as the preceding two examples. Flowers have been added to the sides of her basket, an unusual touch. Made without bocage. Price A. *Elinor Penna.*

Figure 141.13. *Old Ages*. An old lady. Probably made by Dudson. H: 8.9". The brown base and titling are typical of Dudson. Made without bocage. Price A.

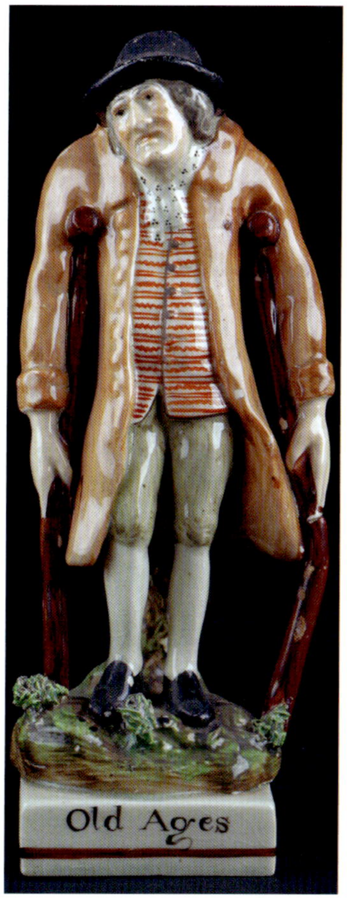

Figure 141.14. *Old Ages*. An old gentleman. Probably made by Dudson. H: 8.4". Companion subject to the previous old lady, but the base is painted in a different typical Dudson manner. Made without bocage. Price A. © *Victoria and Albert Museum, London.*

Figure 141.15. *Old Age, Old Age*. An old lady and an old gentleman, a pair. Probably made by Dudson. H: 9.2". Like the previous examples but titled slightly differently. Made without bocages. Price A. *South Street Antiques, Litchfield, Connecticut.*

Figure 141.16. Old Age, an old lady. H: 5.3". Made without bocage. Price A. *Brighton and Hove Museums*.

Figure 141.17. Old Age, an old gentleman. Attributed to Enoch Wood. H: 5.6". Impressed "18" beneath. Made without bocage. A 5" figure impressed "18" and from the same molds was among Enoch Wood figures of circa 1825 excavated from the Burslem Old Town Hall site. Price A. *Brighton and Hove Museums*.

Figure 141.18. Old Age, an old lady and old gentleman. Attributed to Enoch Wood. H: 7" (L), 7.2" (R). Made without bocages. Both impressed "18" beneath. The gentleman is like the previous gentleman but taller. Price A. *Wisbech & Fenland Museum*.

Figure 141.19. Old Age, reverse of previous pair. The gentleman is 2.2" taller than the matching Enoch Wood excavated figure but has the same impressed number. Enoch Wood apparently made these figures in varying sizes, as he did with some other models. *Wisbech & Fenland Museum*.

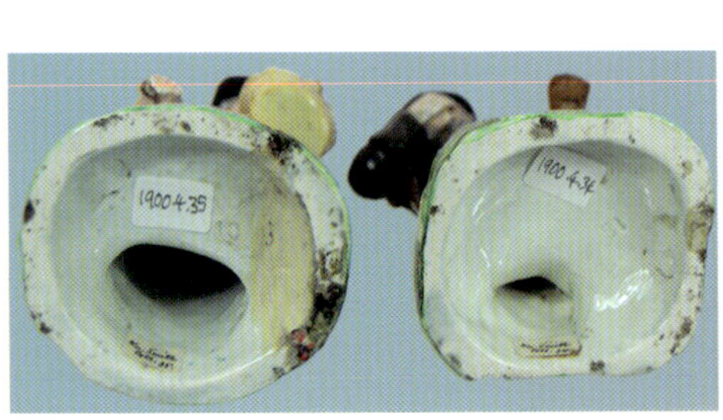

Figure 141.20. Bases of the previous pair of figures of Old Age, with "18" impressed beneath. The thick walls are typical of this type of Enoch Wood base. *Wisbech & Fenland Museum*.

Figure 141.21. Old Age, an old gentleman and an old lady. H: 8.5" (L), 8.3" (R). Made without bocages. Price B. *Elinor Penna*.

Figure 141.22. Old Age, an old gentleman. H: ~7". The base with iron-red double banding is suggestive of "Sherratt" but is insufficient evidence for attribution. Made without bocage. Price A.

Figure 141.23. *AGE, AGE*. An old lady and an old gentleman, a pair. H: 7.2". Made without bocages. Price B. *www.madelena.com*.

Figure 141.24. Old Age, an old lady. H: 7". The disc-shaped base is unusual. Made without bocage. Price A. *Brighton and Hove Museums*.

Figure 141.25. Old Age, a gentleman swathed in a cloak. H: 9.2". An unusual figure, known from only this example. Possibly emblematic of winter. Made without bocage. Price A. *Image courtesy of The Potteries Museum & Art Gallery, Stoke-on-Trent, UK*.

142. Christenings

In the nineteenth century, a christening or baptism was an important life-cycle event marking the existence of what, in those days, might be a very brief life. While the church considered the ceremony a meaningful religious event, many parents christened their babes to protect them from supernatural forces. Superstition dictated that a baby should only be called by name after its christening—prior to that, it was simply called "the baby". Christenings usually took place during Sunday church services, but a sickly baby was christened with great urgency because unchristened children could not be buried in church grounds.

All known christening groups are attributable to "Sherratt," and some are titled *BAPTISM OF MARY*. The group occurs with various "Sherratt" bases and bocages and, on occasion, without a bocage. All have the vicar holding the baby, while the clerk, the father, and two godmothers observe. The mother in most cases did not attend the christening because prior to her "churching" (a simple after-birth thanksgiving ritual during a Sunday church service) she was expected to stay home.

Figure 142.1. *BAPTISM OF MARY*. The vicar (holding the baby), clerk, father, and godmothers; with spill vase and bocage. Attributed to "Sherratt". H: 8". A typical "Sherratt" base and bocage (with oak-leaf fronds and mayflowers). Price D. *Melanie and Nigel Walsh.*

Figure 142.2. Christening. The vicar (holding the baby), clerk, father, and godmothers; with spill vase and bocage. Attributed to "Sherratt". H: 7.6". A typical "Sherratt" base and anthemion bocage fronds Differs from the previous example in that the figures stand on a mound atop the base. Price C. *John Howard; www.antiquepottery.co.uk.*

Figure 142.3. Christening. The vicar (holding the baby), clerk, father, and godmothers; with spill vase and bocage. Attributed to "Sherratt". H: 7.6". The oak leaflet bocage fronds with mayflowers and the feathered base are characteristic of "Sherratt". Price D.

Figure 142.4. *BAPTISM OF MARY*. The vicar (holding the baby), clerk, father, and godmothers; with spill vase and bocage. Attributed to "Sherratt". H: 7.8". On a typical "Sherratt" floral mound base with fern bocage fronds. The floral sprigs applied to the base are exclusive to "Sherratt". Price D.

Figure 142.5. Christening. The vicar (holding the baby), clerk, father, and godmothers, with spill vase. Attributed to "Sherratt". H: 5", L: 7.2". Made without a bocage but has other "Sherratt"-specific characteristics, including the small flowers atop the ladies' bonnets. Price C. *John Howard; www. antiquepottery.co.uk.*

143. Cradles

No evidence supports or contradicts the popular belief that Staffordshire cradles were given as christening gifts. Most of these simple structures tend to date from later in the pre-Victorian decades.

Figure 143.1. Cradle with baby. L: 4.7". Probably made at Bovey Tracey, Devon. Price A. *The William Herbert and Nancy Hunt Collection.*

Figure 143.2. Cradle with child. H: 3.5", L: 9.5". An exceptionally large cradle, and the child is older and better modeled than most. Tassels adorn the pillow. The fingerprints of the worker who dipped the cradle in glaze are evident in the glaze beneath. Price B. *Image courtesy of The Potteries Museum & Art Gallery, Stoke-on-Trent, UK.*

Figure 143.3. Cradle with baby. H: 3", L: 4.5". A well-modeled cradle with larger rockers than most. Price A. *The William Herbert and Nancy Hunt Collection.*

Figure 143.4. Cradle with baby. L: 4.5". Price A. *Martyn Edgell Antiques Ltd.*

Figure 143.5. Cradle with baby. L: 4.3". Price A. *Whitehall Antiques, Chapel Hill, North Carolina.*

Figure 143.6. Cradle with baby. L: 4.2". The pattern on the clothing is suggestive of "Sherratt". Price A. *Michael A. Weinberg, West Pelham Antiques.*

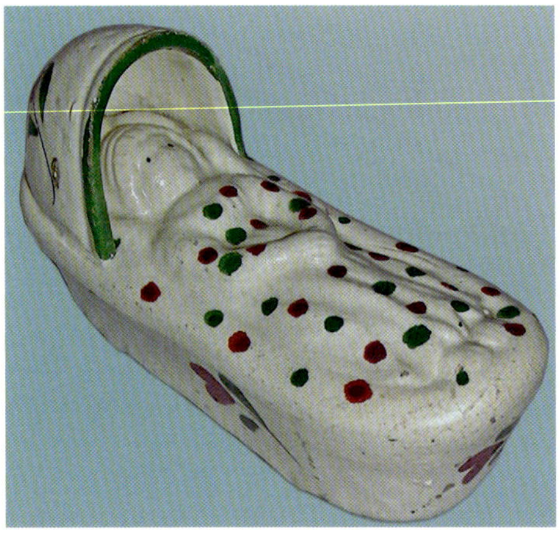

Figure 143.7. Cradle with baby. L: 4". Price A. *Michael A. Weinberg, West Pelham Antiques.*

Figure 143.8. Cradle with baby. L: 4.5". Price A. *John Howard; www.antiquepottery.co.uk.*

Figure 143.9. Cradle with baby. L: 3.8". With enamel and underglaze colors. Price A. *John Howard; www.antiquepottery.co.uk.*

Figure 143.10. Cradle with baby. L: 3". Price A. *John Howard; www.antiquepottery.co.uk.*

Figure 143.11. Cradle with baby. L: 5". Price A. *John Howard; www.antiquepottery.co.uk.*

Figure 143.12. Cradle with baby. L: 4.5". Price A. *John Howard; www.antiquepottery.co.uk.*

Figure 143.13. Cradle. L: 3.5". Price A. *Martyn Edgell Antiques Ltd.*

Figure 143.14. Cradle with baby. L: 7.3". An unusual large model. Price B. *www.madelena.com.*

Figure 143.15. Cradle with baby. L: 7.3". An unusual large model. Price B. *William Herbert and Nancy Hunt Collection.*

144. Parents with Children

Death impacted pre-Victorian family structure in a jarring way. Childbirth, the very foundation of family, was also a mortal peril that routinely ravaged families. High birth rates coupled with high infant and maternal mortality rates made a convoy of cradles and coffins commonplace. But family was then, as it is now, the individual's anchor in life. Heartwarming earthenware domestic scenes seldom fail to bring a smile to the observer's face. These extraordinary figural tableaux are akin to old photographs in an album. They celebrate family and friends of bygone days, and collectors invariably find themselves pondering the identities of those immortalized in clay.

Figure 144.1. Family group, the parents seated on a bench, a baby in her lap and a child on his knee; with bocage. Attributed to "Sherratt". H: 6.2". A rare group, but later, smaller porcelainous examples are more common. The parents and baby are also in "Sherratt" Teetotal groups. Price D.

Figure 144.2. Father with child on his knee. Probably attributable to "Sherratt". H: 5.5". Made without bocage. With losses. From the molds used for the father and child in the previous example. A mother with baby was probably made to pair. Price A. *Peter Flemans.*

Figure 144.3. Mother with a baby on her lap; with bocage. Attributed to "Sherratt". H: 6.3". From molds used in figure 144.1. The companion male figure (with a bocage of the same form) is in the National Trust Collections (no. 118864). Price C.

Figure 144.4. Family group, a man and a lady holding a baby, with cat and dog; with bocage. Attributed to Patriotic Group. H: 8". This base is specific to the Patriotic Group, but the scrolls on it are usually picked out in colors. Price C. *John Howard; www.antiquepottery.co.uk.*

Figure 144.5. Family group, a man and a lady holding a baby, with cat and dog; with bocage. Attributed to Patriotic Group. H: ~8". Like the previous example, but here the bocage fronds comprise hawthorn leaves. These figures occur in other groupings attributable to the same pot bank. Price C.

Figure 144.6. Family group, a man and a lady holding a baby, with cat and dog; with bocage. Attributed to Patriotic Group. H: 7.1". This holly bocage is specific to the Patriotic Group. This pot bank often included both a small cat and dog in groupings. Price C.

Figure 144.7. Family group, a man and a lady holding a baby, with dog, cat, and sheep; with spill vase. Attributed to Patriotic Group. H: ~8.5". The same family as in the previous three examples. This base is specific to the Patriotic Group. Price C. *Elinor Penna.*

Figure 144.8. Family group, a man and a lady holding a baby, with dog, cat, and sheep; with spill vase. Attributed to Patriotic Group. H: 8.5". This man and lady also occur as a pair of figures reading and as musicians on a spill vase. Price C. *Collection of Michael J. Smith.*

Figure 144.9. A mother and child playing pat-a-cake, with a dog and cat at her feet; a mother reading to her child, with a dog at her feet. A pair; with bocages. Attributed to Patriotic Group. H: 8.7" (L), 8.9" (R). The pinecone bocage fronds are specific to the Patriotic Group. Price D.

Figure 144.10. A mother and child playing pat-a-cake, with a dog and cat at her feet; with bocage. Attributed to Patriotic Group. H: ~8.8". Like the previous similar group but with a different bocage that is typical of, yet not specific to, the Patriotic Group. Price C. *John Howard; www.antiquepottery.co.uk.*

Figure 144.11. *PASSTIME*. Mother and child playing pat-a-cake; with bocage. H: 8.7". Attributed to Patriotic Group. Like the previous examples but with the fern leaf bocage fronds sometimes used by the Patriotic Group. Price B. *© Victoria and Albert Museum, London.*

Figure 144.12. *PASTIME*. Mother reading to child; with bocage. H: ~8.7". Attributed to Patriotic Group. This example, like the previous one, lacks the cat and dog seen in figures 144.9-10. The cilantro bocage fronds are typical of the Patriotic Group. Price B.

Figure 144.13. Mother reading to child. H: ~6". Made without bocage. A companion subject to the following example. Price A.

Figure 144.14. Mother and child playing pat-a-cake. H: ~6". Made without bocage. A companion subject to the previous example. Price A.

Figure 144.15. *The Prudent Mother*, a mother reading to a child. Probably made by Enoch Wood. H: 6.4". Impressed "13". After the Derby figure known as *The Prudent Mother*, circa 1780–1790. This figure form was made into the Victorian era. Price B.

Figure 144.16. *Widow & Orphans*. Mother with three children. H: 11". This figure is routinely attributed to John Walton, but not a single marked Walton example substantiates this claim. A large group that is particularly vulnerable to loss. Price B. *John Howard; www.antiquepottery.co.uk.*

Figure 144.17. *MOTHER AND CHILD*. H: ~9". This model would normally be impressed *MADONNA AND CHILD*. Price A.

Figure 144.18. Mother holding child. Height not known. Price A.

Figure 144.19. *My Girl*, published by T. Smyth, circa 1828. This is the design source for figure 144.20. A companion lithograph is titled *My Boy*, but no derivative male figure has yet been recorded.

Figure 144.20. *Ma Bairn* ("my child" in Scots dialect). A plump mother with her tall ungainly daughter. H: 8.7". Known only from this example. The undated satirical lithograph in figure 144.19 is the design source. Price B.

145. Children at Play

In the late eighteenth century, there was growing awareness of childhood as a period of sanctuary before adulthood. Liberal thinkers such as Jean Jacques Rousseau formulated what was to be our modern notion of childhood. At the same time, very many children worked from the tenderest age in England's factories and coal mines, and play was largely the prerogative of the privileged. Earthenware figures give us glimpses of how children played in bygone days. Children then rode upon dogs (shown in Volume 3, chapter 121) and played with iron hoops, but they also enjoyed the simple pleasures of nature and timeless toys, such as dolls.

Figure 145.1. Two boys tussling. H: 5". Possibly made by Enoch Wood. Made without bocage. A variation of the Scuffle/Contest theme. Companion model to figure 147.40. The thick-walled base with a painter's mark beneath is typical of Enoch Wood. Price A.

Figure 145.2. Two children giving alms to a beggar. H: 9.8". No other recorded example. Companion to figure 121.1 (Vol. 3) and has the same bocage. Price C.

Figure 145.3. Boy and girl at play; with bocage. Impressed "WEDGWOOD". H: 7.7". The only recorded example of this group, and the only marked Wedgwood figure with a bocage. Price A.

Figure 145.4. Boy crying, girl holding a bird. A pair. Possibly made by Enoch Wood. H: 7.5" (L), 8.2" (R). The figure of the boy has lost its base, but an example with the same base as on the female figure alongside has been recorded. Price A each. *Brighton and Hove Museums.*

Figure 145.5. Boy crying. Probably made by Enoch Wood. H: 8.7". Like the previous figure of a boy but on a typical Enoch Wood box base. Price A. *Image courtesy of The Potteries Museum & Art Gallery, Stoke-on-Trent, UK.*

Figure 145.6. Girl holding a doll. H: ~5.8". Companion to one of the figures of a boy in his first breeches, following. The sources of these figures are Regency prints titled *See My Baby* (girl figure) and *Just Breeched* (boy figure). Price A.

Figure 145.7. Girl holding a doll. H: 6". With a different head from the previous example and a little larger. This figure appears to be "Sherratt"-like, but nothing supports an attribution. Price A.

Figure 145.8. Boy in his first breeches. H: 6.8". This figure occurs in two sizes, this being the larger. Breeching was the occasion when a young boy abandoned his frock or dress and donned his first breeches. This celebrated rite of passage took place by eight years of age. Price A.

Figure 145.9. Boy in his first breeches. H: 6". This boy is smaller than the preceding example. He stands on a narrower base and may be by a different potter. Price A. *Andrew Dando Antiques.*

Figure 145.10. Boy in his first breeches. H: ~5.2". A different model from previous examples of this subject. Prior to his breeching, a boy wore a dress or pantaloons. These garments were easier to handle, which facilitated toilet training. Price A.

Figure 145.11. Boy with a hoop. Attributed to Blue Group. H: 4.8". Iron hoops, typically made by the local blacksmith, were still seen in England up to the time of World War II. A thin iron rod bent into a hook at its end controlled the hoop. Price A.

Figure 145.12. Reverse of bocage on figure 145.11. These modified fern leaf fronds are specific to the Blue Group.

Figure 145.13. Two girls resting beneath a leafy arbor. H: 4". A pleasing example of a relatively simple group assembled from only two mold parts. Price A. *Andrew Dando Antiques.*

Figure 145.14. Two girls resting beneath a leafy arbor topped by a bocage tree with birds. H: 6.7". Price A.

146. Friendship, Tenderness, Contest, and Scuffle

Groups sometimes titled *Friendship, Tenderness, Contest*, and *Scuffle* are stylistically similar and can be assembled into themed sets, but it is unclear whether they were intended as sets or merely as stand-alone items. The earliest examples are those made by Ralph Wood in the eighteenth century.

The reconciliation between two quarreling lads in Thomas Day's *The History of Sanford and Merton* probably inspired the *Friendship* model. Day's moral children's tale was enjoyed well into the nineteenth century. An engraving from the frontispiece of *The History of Sanford and Merton* (published 1783–1789) may have assisted in the modeling of *Friendship* groups.

Tenderness is the title of a grouping of two people adorning a lamb with a garland. Whereas *Friendship, Contest*, and *Scuffle* groups portray children, most *Tenderness* show a more mature couple.

Groups of children at play are sometimes titled *Scuffle* and *Contest*. Knowing which is which is impossible as the titles were used interchangeably. *Contest* and *Scuffle* possibly have a design source because an earlier oak wood panel sold at auction bore a similar design.[1]

Figure 146.1. *Friendſhip, Tenderness, Scuffle, Contest.* Four companion groups, each with bocage. Scuffle impressed "Ra. Wood Burslem"; *Tenderness* impressed "W.". All made by or attributed to Ralph Wood. Price C. *Collection of Michael J. Smith.*

Figure 146.2. Engraving from *The History of Sanford and Merton, after Thomas Stothard, 1783–1789*. Possibly the design source for Friendship.

Figure 146.3. Friendship. Two boys arm in arm, with dog; with bocage. Attributed to Ralph Wood; impressed "154". H: 5.5". Price A. *Michael Goodacre*.

Figure 146.4. *Friendship*. Two boys arm in arm, with dog; with bocage. Attributed to Ralph Wood. H: 6.9". A similar group is recorded with "W" impressed on the back of the base. Price A.

Figure 146.5. *Friendship*. Two boys arm in arm, with dog. Attributed to Ralph Wood. H: ~6.5". The titling, painting of the base, and color palette are typical of slightly later Ralph Wood figures. Bocage lost. Price A. *Bardith Ltd*.

Figure 146.6. Friendship. Two boys arm in arm, with dog; with bocage. Possibly made by Dudson. H: 7.1". The bocage (with losses) is suggestive of Dudson. Price A. *The Bowes Museum, Barnard Castle*.

Figure 146.7. Friendship. Two boys arm in arm; with bocage. Attributed to Dudson. H: ~7.3". A typical Dudson bocage and base. A dog may be lost from the base. Price A.

Figure 146.8. *Friendship*. Two boys arm in arm, with dog; with bocage. Impressed "WALTON". H: 7.4". The rosette molded into the center front of the base occurs only on marked Walton figures. Price B.

Figure 146.9. Friendship. Two boys arm in arm, with dog; with bocage. H: ~7". A companion to the following Tenderness, having the same base and bocage. Price A.

Figure 146.10. Tenderness. A couple placing a garland on a sheep; with bocage. H: ~7". From the same unknown pot bank as the previous Friendship group. Price A.

Figure 146.11. *Friendship*. Two boys arm in arm, with dog; with bocage. H: ~8". Tenderness, Contest and Scuffle groups occur on similarly titled and decorated bases. Price B. *John Howard; www.antiquepottery.co.uk.*

Figure 146.12. *Tendernefs*. A couple placing a garland on a sheep. Attributed to Ralph Wood; impressed "153". H: 6.1". Bocage lost. Stoneware/porcelainous body. Several Wood groups occur with a somewhat more vitreous body, indicating experimentation with different clays. Price A.

Figure 146.13. *Tenderness*. A couple placing a garland on a sheep; with bocage. Attributed to Ralph Wood, impressed "W". H: ~6.4". Enoch Wood also impressed letters onto some of his figures, but here multiple other features support the Ralph Wood attribution. Price A.

Figure 146.14. *Tenderness*. A couple placing a garland on a sheep; with bocage. Attributed to Ralph Wood. H: ~6.5". Ralph Wood figures tend to have small bocages, and it is difficult to find one in good condition. Price A.

Figure 146.15. Tenderness. A couple placing a garland on a sheep; with bocage. Attributed to Dudson. H: ~6". Price B. *Andrew Dando Antiques.*

Figure 146.16. Tenderness. A couple placing a garland on a sheep; with bocage. Attributed to Dudson. H: ~6". Price A.

Figure 146.17. Tenderness. A couple placing a garland on a sheep; with bocage. Attributed to Dudson. H: ~6". This example was made without the square base used for previously shown examples of this group. Price A.

Figure 146.18. *TENDERNESS*. A couple placing a garland on a sheep; with bocage. H: 8.3". Superior enamels and glazes and a dazzling bocage. Bocages with these leaflets arranged in threes consistently appear on an unclassified array of figures from the same pot bank. Price C.

Figure 146.19. *TENDERNESS*. A couple placing a garland on a sheep; with bocage. H: ~8.3". From the same molds as the previous example. Price B.

Figure 146.20. Tenderness. A couple placing a garland on a sheep; with bocage. H: 8". Price A.

Figure 146.21. Tenderness. A couple placing a garland on a sheep; with bocage. H: ~10". Similar groups with tall bocages with birds show the couple holding a bird or bird's nest (chapter 147). The base is replaced. Price A.

Figure 146.22. *TENDERNESS*. A couple placing a garland on a sheep; with bocage. Impressed "WALTON". H: 7". Reproductions of this group abound. They are characterized by lack-luster modeling and sanserif letters for the title and the Walton mark. Price B. *John Howard; www.antiquepottery.co.uk*.

Figure 146.23. *TENDERNESS*. A couple placing a garland on a sheep; with bocage. Impressed "WALTON". H: 7.7". Walton groups with full, fine bocages are particularly pleasing. Price B.

Figure 146.24. *TENDERNESS*. A couple placing a garland on a sheep; with bocage. H: ~7.5". Unmarked but in the style of Walton. The rosette normally found modeled into the center front of the base of Walton versions is not present, and this group probably was not made by Walton. Price B.

Figure 146.25. *Scuffle*. Boy and two girls playing, a hat at their feet. Attributed to Ralph Wood; impressed "131". H: 6.5". The bocage is lost. Price A. *Image courtesy of The Potteries Museum & Art Gallery, Stoke-on-Trent, UK.*

Figure 146.26. *Scuffle*. Boy and two girls playing, he holds a hat; with bocage. Impressed "Ra. Wood Burslem". H: ~7". A different composition from the previous example with the same title. The base, titling, palette, and bocage are typical of Ralph Wood. Price A.

Figure 146.27. *Contest*. Boy and two girls playing, he holds a hat; with bocage. Attributed to Ralph Wood, impressed "133". H: 7.1". Like the Scuffle in figure 146.26 but now titled Contest. A stoneware/porcelainous body. Price A. *Image courtesy of The Potteries Museum & Art Gallery, Stoke-on-Trent, UK.*

Figure 146.28. *Contest, Scuffle*. Boy and two girls playing, a hat in his hand in one group, a hat on the ground in the other group, a pair with bocages. Attributed to Ralph Wood, impressed "133" (L) and "134" (R). H: 8.2". Price B. *Bardith Ltd.*

Figure 146.29. *Contest*. Boy and two girls playing, a hat at their feet; with bocage. Attributed to Ralph Wood. H: ~8". This larger lettering occurs on some Ralph Wood titles. Price A.

Figure 146.30. *Scuffle*. Boy and two girls playing, he holds a hat; with bocage. Attributed to Ralph Wood. H: 7.7". Price A.

Figure 146.31. *Contest*. Boy and two girls playing, a hat at their feet; with bocage. Attributed to Ralph Wood. H: 7.7". Price A. *Brighton and Hove Museums*.

Figure 146.32. Contest or Scuffle. Boy and two girls playing, he holds a hat; with bocage. H: ~7.7". This bocage and double-lined base occur on other figure groups. Price A.

Figure 146.33. *Scuffle*. Boy and two girls playing, a hat at their feet; with bocage. H: 7.7". This unusual form of titling is seen on figure 26.108 in Volume 1. Price B. *Image courtesy of The Potteries Museum & Art Gallery, Stoke-on-Trent, UK.*

Figure 146.34. Contest or Scuffle. Boy and two girls playing, he holds a hat; with bocage. Attributed to Dudson. H: ~7.2". The brown base and the bocage are typical of Dudson. Hat restored. Price A.

Figure 146.35. *Contest*. Boy and two girls playing, he holds a hat; with bocage. Attributed to Dudson. H: 7.2". The bocage and the brown base with its titling are typical of Dudson. Price A. *Aurea Carter Antiques.*

Figure 146.36. *Contest*. Boy and two girls playing, he holds a hat; with bocage. Attributed to Dudson. H: ~7.5". Similar to the previous Dudson groups, but the base is painted and titled in another typical Dudson style. Price A.

Figure 146.37. Contest or Scuffle. Boy and two girls playing, he holds a hat; with bocage. Attributed to Dudson. H: 8.3". The bocage is consistent with the attribution. Price A. *The Bowes Museum, Barnard Castle.*

Figure 146.38. Contest or Scuffle. Boy and two girls playing, a hat at their feet; with bocage. H: 7.5". These three-leaflet bocage fronds occur on other fine figures, as yet unclassified. Price B.

Figure 146.39. *CONTEST*. Boy and two girls playing, he holds a hat; with bocage. H: 7.5". A companion to the previous example, having the same bocage fronds but the base is painted in a vermicular pattern. Such bases and bocage fronds often occur in combination. Price B.

Figure 146.40. Detail of the three-leaflet bocage fronds on figure 146.39.

Figure 146.41. *SCUFFLE, CONTEST*. Boy and two girls playing, a hat at their feet in one group, a hat on the ground in the other group, a pair with bocages. H: 7.5". With three-leaflet bocage fronds and probably from the same pot bank as figures 146.38 and 146.39. Price B.

Figure 146.42. Scuffle and Contest. Boy and two girls playing, a hat in his hand in one group, a hat at their feet in the other group, a pair with bocages. Attributed to Big Blossom Group. H: 7.8". Strikingly painted bases with typical big blossoms on the bocages. Price B.

Scuffle and Contest, reverse of previous pair.

Figure 146.44. Scuffle or Contest. Boy and two girls playing, a hat at their feet; with bocage. Impressed "WALTON". H: 8.2". The base is reminiscent of that on other Walton groups. Companion to the following group. Price B.

Figure 146.45. Scuffle or Contest. Boy and two girls playing, he holds a hat; with bocage. Impressed "WALTON". H: 8.7". Companion to the previous group. Price B. *Elinor Penna.*

Figure 146.46. Scuffle or Contest. Boy and two girls playing, a hat at their feet; with bocage. H: ~8.6". Like marked Walton groups, but unmarked and lacking typical Walton decoration. The rosette molded into the base of Walton examples is not present. Price B. *John Howard; www.antiquepottery.co.uk.*

147. Bird Nesters and Nut Gatherers

Nineteenth-century children enjoyed the ancient childhood pastimes of collecting nuts and birds' eggs. These hobbies required nothing but innate curiosity, so young princes and paupers alike scaled trees and wormed through hedges in pursuit of nature's treasures. Nostalgic renditions of children engaged in these pursuits recall the habits and pleasures of a bygone era.

Figure 147.1. *BIRDS NEST, BIRDS NEST*. Boy and girl each holding a bird and eggs in a hat, a pair, each with bocage. Impressed "SALT". H: 6.2". Price B.

Figure 147.2. *BIRDS NEST,* reverse of previous pair showing the "Salt" mark on each.

Figure 147.3. *BIRDS NEST*. Girl holding a bird and eggs; with bocage. H~6". With a Salt-type bocage but not attributable. Price A.

Figure 147.4. *BIRDS NEST*. Girl holding a bird and eggs; with bocage. H: 5.1". With a Salt-type bocage, but blue carnations are not recorded on marked Salt figures. The combination of flower colors is suggestive of Hall. Price A. *Michael Goodacre*.

Figure 147.5. *BIRDS NEST*. Boy holding a bird and eggs; with bocage. Impressed "HALL". H: ~6". Price A.

Figure 147.6. *BIRDS NEST*. Boy holding a bird and eggs; with bocage. Impressed "HALL". H: 6.1". Carnations (red or blue) with large yellow centers are typical of Hall. The figure seems to be from the same molds as the similar Salt figure (fig. 147.1). Price B.

Figure 147.7. *BIRDS NEST*, reverse of previous figure showing Hall's mark impressed directly into the body.

Figure 147.8. Girl with a nest; with bocage. Possibly made by Walton. H: ~5.3". Her right arm held a bird, now lost. Unmarked and from the same molds as figure 147.9, marked "WALTON". Price A.

Figure 147.9. Girl with a bird and nest; with bocage. Impressed "WALTON". H: 5.3". Price A. *Peter Flemans*.

Figure 147.10. Girl holding a bird and nest; with bocage. Impressed "WALTON". H: 6". This figure has the same head as the previous Walton figure, but the body and base utilize different molds. Companion to figure 147.12. Price A.

Figure 147.11. Girl holding a bird and nest; with bocage. Possibly made by Walton. H: 6.2". Unmarked, but close similarities to figure 147.10 suggest the attribution. Price A. *Barbara Gair; www.castle-antiques.com*

Figure 147.12. Boy holding a bird and nest; with bocage. Impressed "WALTON". H: 6". Companion to figure 147.10. Price A. *Brighton and Hove Museums*.

Figure 147.13. Boy holding a bird and nest; with bocage. Impressed "WALTON". H: 5.6". Like the previous figure but on a different and lower base. Price A.

Figure 147.14. Boy holding a bird and nest; with bocage. Possibly made by Walton. H: 5.7". Like figure 147.12 but unmarked and utilizes a different mold for the base. Price A. *Elinor Penna*.

Figure 147.15. *BIRD WSST* (misspelled, partially impressed). Girl holding a bird and eggs; with bocage. H: ~6". Price A.

Figure 147.16. Girl holding a bird; with bocage. Attributed to "Sherratt". H: ~4.3". Typical "Sherratt" bocage. Companion subject to figure 147.18. Price A.

Figure 147.17. Girl holding a bird; with bocage. Attributed to "Sherratt". H: 4.3". Like the previous figure but with different bocage flowers and base. Companion subject to the following boy. Price A.

Figure 147.18. Boy holding a bird and nest; with bocage. Attributed to "Sherratt". H: ~4.3". Companion subject to figures 147.16–17. Price A.

Figure 147.19. Boy holding a nest; with bocage. H: ~6.3". This figure most commonly occurs without a bocage. Price A.

Figure 147.20. Boy holding a nest. H: 5.3". Like the previous figure but with a low green stump rather than a bocage. Price A. *Brighton and Hove Museums.*

Figure 147.21. Boy holding a nest. H: ~5.3". Made without bocage. Price A. *Andrew Dando Antiques.*

Figure 147.22. Boy holding a nest. H: 5.3". Made without bocage. Like the previous examples but on a brown base. Price A. *Elinor Penna.*

Figure 147.23. Boy holding a nest. Attributed to Gray Base Group. H: ~5.3". Probably made without bocage. Price A.

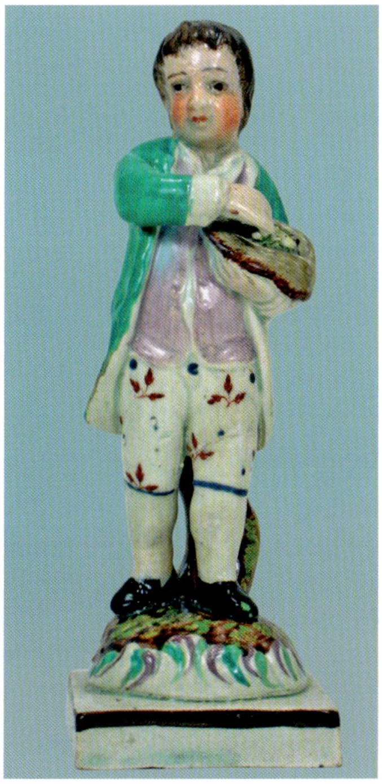

Figure 147.24. Boy holding a nest. H: ~5.3". Made without bocage. Pairs with figure 114.18 in Volume 3. Price A.

Figure 147.25. Boy holding a nest. H: ~6". Made without bocage. This figure is from different molds than figures 147.19–24. His right hand and arm are restored. Price A.

Figure 147.26. Boy holding a bird and nest, girl holding a flower, a pair. H: 5.5" (L); 5.8" (R). Made without bocages. The thick-walled bases are suggestive of an Enoch Wood origin. Price B.

Figure 147.27. Lady holding a bird and nest. H: 5.8". Companion to one or other of the following two figures. All are uncommon. Price A. *Collection of Michael J. Smith*.

Figure 147.28. Gentleman holding a bird and nest. H: 5.8". Three other figures are recorded on this base: a figure of Madame Vestris, and the preceding and following figures. Price A.

Figure 147.29. Gentleman holding a bird and nest. H: 6". The molds from the previous figure have been adapted to yield this more wooden depiction. Price A.

Figure 147.30. Gentleman holding a bird and nest, reverse of the previous two figures showing the differences in the modelling.

Figure 147.31. Boy holding a nest, with dog; with bocage. Attributed to Ralph Wood. H: 6.7". The bocage, the flowers, the line around three sides of the base, and the rainbow palette of the base mound are typical of Ralph Wood. The boy and the dog are also on a Ralph Wood spill vase (fig. 147.53). Price A.

Figure 147.32. Boy climbing a tree, with squirrel and dog; with bocage. Attributed to Patriotic Group. H: ~6". The base and bocage flowers are characteristic of the Patriotic Group. Companion to the following example. Price A.

Figure 147.33. Boy holding a nest, with dog; with bocage. H: ~6". Attributed to Patriotic Group. Companion to the previous example. Price A.

Figure 147.34. Boy holding a nest, with dog; with bocage. H: 6.4". Attributed to Patriotic Group. Price A. *Elinor Penna*.

Figure 147.35. Boy holding a nest, with dog; with bocage. Attributed to Dudson. H: 5.5". The bocage supports the attribution. Price A. *Brighton and Hove Museums*.

Figure 147.36. Boy holding a nest, with dog; with bocage. H: 6". These three-leaflet bocage fronds occur repeatedly on fine figures that are as yet unclassified. Price B.

Figure 147.37. Boy climbing a tree, with squirrel and hat; with bocage. Attributed to Dudson. H: ~6". The bocage is typical of Dudson. Price A.

Figure 147.38. Boy climbing a tree, with squirrel, dog, and hat; with bocage. H: ~6". As in other similar groups, the hat holds nuts. These three-leaflet bocage fronds are typical of an unclassified array of figures from the same source. Price B.

Figure 147.39. Boy climbing a tree, with squirrel, dog, and hat; with bocage. H: 6.5". Price B.

Figure 147.40. Two boys tussling over a nest. H: 5". Possibly made by Enoch Wood. A variation of the Scuffle/Contest theme. Like the following example but made without bocage. Companion model to figure 145.1. The thick-walled base is typical of Enoch Wood. Price A.

Figure 147.41. Two boys tussling over a nest. H: 4.8". Possibly made by Enoch Wood. Like the previous example but made with a typical Enoch Wood bocage. Price A.

Figure 147.42. Gentleman holding a bird, lady holding a nest; with bocage. H: 10.2". The bocage leaves are single sided, i.e. each leaf is not paired back-to-back with another. Price B. *Woolley & Wallis Salisbury Salerooms Ltd.*

Figure 147.43. Gentleman and lady, each holding a bird, with two sheep and a goat, with a bocage with birds. Impressed "WALTON". H: 9.1". An uncommon group. Groups titled *Tenderness* look rather similar and incorporate the same couple in a different setting. Price C. *Brighton and Hove Museums*.

Figure 147.44. Gentleman and lady, each holding a bird, with a sheep, with a bocage with birds. H: 10.5". A stunning example, with a very tall bocage comprising three-leaflet fronds. Uses the figures that are in Tenderness groups. Price C. *Brighton and Hove Museums*.

Figure 147.45. Lady and gentleman, each holding a bird, with a sheep, with a bocage with birds. H: ~9.2". With the same bocage fronds as the previous group and possibly from the same pot bank. The figures have switched positions. Price B.

Figure 147.46. Gentleman and lady, each holding a bird, with a hat holding fledglings, with a bocage with birds. H: 9.7". The same distinctive bocage fronds as on figures 147.48–50, all probably from the same pot bank. The lady's upper body and head differ from those in the other similar groups. Price B.

Figure 147.47. Gentleman and lady, each holding a bird, with a hat holding fledglings, with a bocage with birds. H: ~9.7". Note the distinctive bocage. Price B.

Figure 147.48. Gentleman and lady, each holding a bird, with a hat holding fledglings; with a bocage with birds. H: 9.7". The bocage, like that on the previous and following similar examples, has round five-petalled flowers integral to it. All groups are from the same pot bank. Price B.

Figure 147.49. Detail of the reverse of the bocage on the previous example. The flowers integral to the leaves are not picked out in colors on the back of the bocage.

Figure 147.50. Lady and gentleman, each holding a bird, with a hat holding fledglings; with a bocage with birds. H: ~9.7". Like the previous group but the figures have switched positions. Price B.

Figure 147.51. Two large canaries, two fledglings, and a tiny man perched in a bocage, with two sheep. H: 8.2". This fanciful group is possibly unique. Price C. *Brighton and Hove Museums.*

Figure 147.52. Boy climbing a tree; with a spill vase with a nest. H: 10.5". Price A. *Elinor Penna.*

Figure 147.53. Boy seated with a dog and holding a nest; with a spill vase with a bird. Attributed to Ralph Wood; impressed "164". H: 8.7". Price A. *Whitehall Antiques, Chapel Hill, North Carolina.*

Figure 147.54. Base of previous example showing "164" impressed in the base. *Whitehall Antiques, Chapel Hill, North Carolina.*

Figure 147.55. Left: Boy climbing a tree; with a spill vase with a nest. Right: Boy seated with a dog and holding a nest; with a spill vase with a bird. A pair. Possibly made by Ralph Wood. H: ~10". The example on the right uses the same molds as the Ralph Wood example impressed "164" (fig. 147.53). Price B.

Figure 147.56. Boy climbing a tree; with a spill vase with a squirrel. Possibly made by Ralph Wood. H: ~10.5". The similarity to the example in the figure 147.55 and the rainbow palette of the base suggest the attribution. Price A. *www.madelena.com.*

Figure 147.57. Boy seated at the base of a tree holding a nest; with spill vase. H: 8.8". Price A. *Elinor Penna*.

Figure 147.58. Boy reclining at the base of a tree; with spill vase with a bird. H: ~10". Price B. *John Howard; www.antiquepottery.co.uk.*

Figure 147.59. Boy seated at the base of tree and holding a nest, with two dogs; with spill vase with a bird. H: 8.7". Losses and restoration to spill vase. Price A. *Photograph Courtesy of Sotheby's, Inc. © 2014.*

Figure 147.60. Boy climbing a tree, with two leopards and a dog; with a spill vase with a squirrel. H: 8.4". Price C. *Elinor Penna*.

Figure 147.61. Boy climbing a tree, with two leopards; with a spill vase with a squirrel. H: 8.6". Like the previous example but painted differently and with flowers strewn on the base. Price C. *Collection of Arnold and Barbara Berlin.*

Figure 147.62. Boy climbing a tree, with two leopards (each with a bocage) and a dog; with a spill vase with a squirrel. H: ~8.6". Price C.

Figure 147.63. Boy climbing a tree, with two sheep (each with a bocage) and a dog; with a spill vase with a squirrel. H: ~8.6". Boy not original to the group. Price B.

Figure 147.64. Boy climbing a tree, with two deer (each with a bocage); with a spill vase with a squirrel. H: ~8.6". Both bocages are restored. Price B.

148. The Temperance Movement

In the early 1800s, Britain wallowed in an epidemic of disruptive public drunkenness. Because water supplies were contaminated, beer was the safest, most palatable drink. The Temperance Movement, established circa 1828, proposed eliminating drunkenness by encouraging the drinking of beer instead of spirits. But drinking lots of beer did not keep the public sober, so the Teetotal Movement, established circa 1832, promoted total abstinence from all alcohol.[1]

The most well-known earthenware figure groups related to temperance are the "Sherratt" groups usually titled *ALE BENCH* and *TEE TOTAL* that date from around 1830. In their three forms, the groups (two models titled *ALE BENCH* and one titled *TEE TOTAL*) mirror the progression of the temperance movement.

1. ***ALE BENCH***, showing a couple happily drinking ale (fig. 148.1). The early temperance movement encouraged beer drinking because beer was thought to be a wholesome substitute for more intoxicating beverages.
2. ***ALE BENCH***, showing a violent fight between a man and lady (fig. 148.3). People soon realized that drinking beer to excess could be just as intoxicating as drinking any other form of alcohol and it perpetuated the cycle of public and domestic violence.
3. ***TEE TOTAL***, showing a family happily partaking of tea while the father clutches his head—a hangover perhaps (figs. 148.4–6)? Teetotalism encouraged abandoning all alcohol and drinking tea instead.

These groups were probably originally sold individually, and buyers—then or subsequently—sometimes paired them. Of the three groups, the *ALE BENCH* showing a fight is the rarest. The groups can be dated to post 1828, and they are always on either marbled footed table bases or, more rarely, on marbled flat bases. Interestingly, not one is recorded on the familiar "Sherratt" brown base with clawed feet, suggesting that this base was being phased out by that time. Titles are sometimes placed twice on the apron of the base. It is speculated that these double-titled groups are slightly earlier than those with a single title. Perhaps "Sherratt" came to realize that symmetry could be maintained by simply positioning one title in the center of the apron on the base.

"Sherratt" also made a drinking scene that is not fashioned as the conventional *ALE BENCH* (fig. 148.7). This group is known from one example, and, because it is on a brown base with claw feet, it may predate all groups on marbled bases. It uses the same figure molds as the *ALE BENCH* model in figure 148.1 and may have been its precursor.

Several other pot banks fashioned drinking groups very like the "Sherratt" drinking scene on a brown base (figs. 148.8–17). Some pot banks made two compositions that were probably intended to pair. In one, the couple is happily glugging away. In the other, the couple is fighting and a bag (perhaps a money bag) is behind the man's feet. These two groups show the opposing perspectives on beer: a source of health and contentment, or a cause of family violence.

Figure 148.1. *ALE BENCH, ALE BENCH*. Man and lady sitting around a table drinking; with spill vase and bocage. Attributed to "Sherratt". H: 8.4". The small table on this group is routinely missing or restored. The bocage, base, turret spill vase, dress patterns, and titling are typical of Sherratt. Price D.

Figure 148.2. *ALE BENCH, ALE BENCH*, reverse of previous example.

Figure 148.3. *ALE BENCH*. Man and lady fighting, a table upturned; with spill vase and bocage. Attributed to "Sherratt". H: 8". This "fighting ale bench" is the scarcest of the three "Sherratt" temperance groups on table bases. Examples of this group and *TEE TOTAL* are recorded decorated with pink luster. Price D.

Figure 148.4. *TEE TOTAL, TEE TOTAL*. Man and lady with baby at the tea table; with spill vase and bocage. Attributed to "Sherratt". H: 8". This group, although difficult to procure, occurs more frequently than either of the ALE BENCH groups. Price D. *Andrew Dando Antiques*.

Figure 148.5. *TEE TOTAL*. Man and lady with baby at the tea table; with spill vase and bocage. Attributed to "Sherratt". H: 8.1". Very like the previous example, but the title appears only once on the apron of the base. Price D.

Figure 148.6. *TEE TOTAL*. Man and lady with baby at the tea table; with spill vase and bocage. Attributed to "Sherratt". H: 7". This uncommon base also occurs on "Sherratt" *ALE BENCH* and *TAM O'SHANTER SOUTER JOHNNY* groups. Price D. *Collection of Michael J. Smith*.

Figure 148.7. Drinking group, lady and man fight as she drinks; with bocage. Attributed to "Sherratt". H: ~9". Restored bocage. A companion to the "Sherratt" group on a brown table base titled *COURT SHIP* (fig. 138.11). Each is known from only one example. Price A.

Figure 148.8. Drinking group, lady and man fight as she drinks; with bocage. Possibly attributable to "Sherratt". H: ~8". With losses. "Sherratt" and other pot banks used this bocage. Companion to a similar untitled courtship group (fig. 138.12). Price B.

Figure 148.9. Drinking group, lady and man drink companionably; with bocage. H: 8". Companion to the following group. Price A. *Elinor Penna*.

Figure 148.10. Drinking group, lady and man fight as she drinks; with bocage. H: 7.9". Companion to the preceding group. Price A. *Elinor Penna*.

Figure 148.11. Drinking group, lady and man drink companionably; with bocage. Attributed to Tunstall Group. H: 8.7". The bocage (including flowers) is characteristic of Tunstall. The back of this group is unpainted. Price A. *Brighton and Hove Museums*.

Figure 148.12. Drinking group, reverse of previous example showing the unpainted back, as sometimes occurs on Tunstall examples. *Brighton and Hove Museums*.

Figure 148.13. Drinking group, lady and man drink companionably; with bocage. Attributed to Tunstall Group. H: ~8.7". Like the previous example but painted differently. Price B. *John Howard; www.antiquepottery.co.uk.*

Figure 148.14. Drinking group, lady and man drink companionably; with bocage. Attributed to Tunstall Group. H: ~8.7". A companion to a similarly decorated courtship group (fig. 138.14). Price A.

Figure 148.15. Drinking group, lady and man drink companionably; with bocage. Attributed to Tunstall Group. H: 8.7". Like previous Tunstall examples but painted differently. Price B.

Figure 148.16. Drinking group, lady and man fight as she drinks; with bocage. H: 6.7". The small dog on groups of this sort is frequently lost. Price B.

Figure 148.17. Drinking group, lady and man fight as she drinks; with bocage. H: 6.7". Price B. *Collection of Michael J. Smith.*

149. Buildings

Figure 149.1. House. H: 2.7", L: 3". Made without bocage. On the reverse, the house and the base are both flat, and the house is unpainted. Price A.

Figure 149.2. House in pastoral setting, with a cow and a sheep; with bocage. H: 4.1", L: 6.3". The house is molded like the house in the previous example. Price A. *Elinor Penna*.

Figure 149.3. House in pastoral setting, with a woman, a cow and a sheep; with bocage. H: 3.1". The house is from the same molds as the previous two houses. Price B. *Collection of Arnold & Barbara Berlin.*

Figure 149.4. House in pastoral setting, with two sheep; with bocage. H: 3.3". On the reverse, the house is flat and unpainted, but the base is rounded and fully painted. Price B.

Figure 149.5. House; with bocage. H: 3.6". The house is flat and painted on the reverse. Price B.

Figure 149.6 .House, reverse of previous example.

Figure 149.7. House. L: 3". The house and base are flat and unpainted on the reverse. Price A. *Collection of Barbara Hunt Crow.*

Figure 149.8. Turreted cottage, with a sheep; with bocage. Possibly by "Sherratt". H: ~4". The bocage and color palette suggest the attribution. Price A.

Figure 149.9. Whimsical house atop a bridge, with man blowing a horn, four sheep and a duck; with bocage. Possibly by "Sherratt". H: ~8". The modeling and turquoise palette hint at a "Sherratt" attribution. Price A.

Figure 149.10. Whimsical house atop a bridge, with five sheep and two swans; with bocage. H: ~6". From molds used for the previous example. Price A. *Collection of Arnold & Barbara Berlin.*

Figure 149.11. Church, with two gentlemen and two cows; with bocage. H: ~5.3". The back of this group is flat. Price B.

Figure 149.12. House. H: 3.1", L: 4.3". Made without bocage. On the reverse, the house and base are both flat and unpainted. The chimney was lost in manufacture. The color palette is suggestive of the northeast pot banks. Price A.

Figure 149.13. Folly with thatched roof, with two naked cherubs and a flower pot; with bocage. H: 3.5". Price C.

Figure 149.14. Cottage-style money box. H: 3.7". Price A. *John Howard; www.antiquepottery.co.uk.*

Figure 149.15. Square turret formed as a spill vase on a flower-strewn mound. H: 5.3", L: 7.1". Price A. *www.madelena.com.*

Figure 149.16. Turret atop a bridge, a boat beneath. Impressed "WALTON". H: 5.7". Price A. *Andrew Dando Antiques.*

Figure 149.17. Church with two tombstones in the churchyard. L: 6.8". Decorated with pink luster. Price C. *John Howard; www.antiquepottery.co.uk.*

Figure 149.18. House. H: 9", L: 8". The roof lifts off. Price C. *John Howard; www.antiquepottery.co.uk.*

Figure 149.19. Cottage formed as a pastille burner, with five animals; with bocage. H: ~6". Dudson made similarly styled cottages, but there is no basis for attributing this example. Price A.

Figure 149.20. Cottage formed as a pastille burner. H: ~4.2". Made without bocage. A simpler version of the previous cottage. Price A.

Figure 149.21. Cottage formed as a pastille burner. H: 3.3". Impressed "R" beneath twice. Price A. *Whitehall Antiques, Chapel Hill, North Carolina.*

Figure 149.22. New Hall (originally known as Shelton Hall), Shelton, formed as a pastille burner. L: 13.5". Possibly made by Hollins, Warburton & Co., which operated at New Hall and is better known for its porcelain. The same pastille burner was made in porcelain. Price D. © *Christie's Images Limited 2014.*

Figure 149.23. Castle. L: 13.5". After Stafford Castle. The structure is open from the top and could have held flowers within the turrets and keep. Another in the Earle Collection from the same molds but with a clock face and loose spire added portrays a church. Price C. *The William Herbert and Nancy Hunt Collection.*

Figure 149.24. Castle spill holder. L: 8.2". Price A. *The William Herbert and Nancy Hunt Collection.*

Figure 149.26. Three terrace house, a component of the remarkable toy village in figure 149.25.

Figure 149.25. Toy village. Four three-house terraces L: 4" with "37" painted beneath two; two-house terrace L. 2.6" with "27" painted beneath; town hall/ market H: 3.5" with "21" painted beneath; church H: 3.5" and painted "19" or "61" beneath; windmill H: 21" and painted "27" beneath; and gate L: 1.6". Price E, set.

150. Mansion House Dwarves.

Dwarves who stood outside London's Mansion House (the Lord Mayor's official residence) with advertisements pinned to their large hats were called Mansion House dwarves. English porcelain factories fashioned Mansion House dwarves in figural form after engravings of dwarf entertainers by the French engraver Jacques Callot (1592–1635).

Figure 150.1. A pair of Mansion House dwarves. Possibly made by Enoch Wood. H: 6.7" (L), 6.1" (R). The bases and the flowers on them are in the style of Enoch Wood. Price B. *Wisbech & Fenland Museum.*

Figure 150.2. Reverse of previous Mansion House dwarves. Note the advertisements pinned to the clothing of the dwarf on the right. *Wisbech & Fenland Museum*

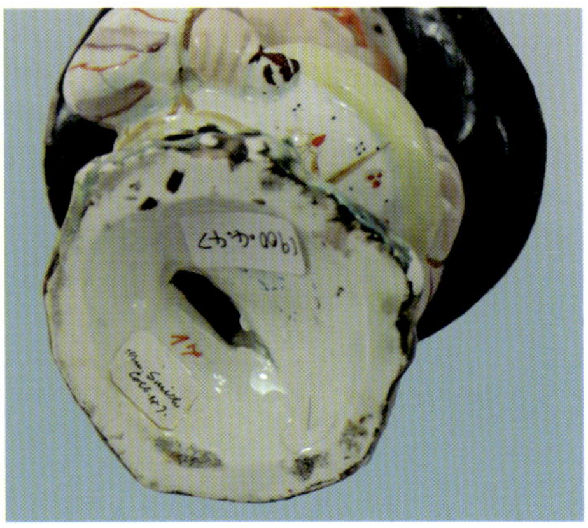

Figure 150.3. Base of a Mansion House dwarf in the previous example. All recorded Mansion House dwarves have such bases, which are consistent with an Enoch Wood attribution. *Wisbech & Fenland Museum.*

Figure 150.4. Mansion House dwarf. Possibly made by Enoch Wood. H: 6.2". Unlike previous examples, the base is undecorated, but it is formed in the manner of Enoch Wood bases. Price A. *John Howard; www.antiquepottery.co.uk.*

Figure 150.5. Mansion House dwarf. Possibly made by Enoch Wood. H: 6.4". Like all recorded examples, this figure has an Enoch Wood-type base. Price A. *The Bowes Museum, Barnard Castle.*

151. Roger Giles.

Crudely comical figures of a squatting gentleman formed as a pepper pot are said to represent Roger Giles. Giles was a Devonshire schoolteacher who reportedly advertised on a signboard to sell fresh eggs "new laid by him every day". The date of the advertisement is not known, but these Roger Giles pots place the hitherto-undated Roger Giles yarn into the pre-Victorian era. All recorded examples are made without bocages.

Figure 151.1. Roger Giles. Attributed to "Sherratt". H: 4.7". The base is specific to "Sherratt". Price A.

Figure 151.2. Roger Giles, reverse of previous figure.

Figure 151.3. Roger Giles. Attributed to "Sherratt". H: ~4.7". Price A.

Figure 151.4. Roger Giles. H: ~4.7". Price A. *Andrew Dando Antiques.*

Figure 151.5. Roger Giles. H: 4.7". Price A. *Peter Flemans.*

Figure 151.6. Roger Giles. H: 4.3". Price A. *Collection of Arnold and Barbara Berlin.*

Figure 151.7. Roger Giles. H: 3.8". Price A. *Andrew Dando Antiques.*

152. The Welsh Tailor and his Wife

Figures of a man and lady astride goats represent the Welsh tailor and his wife. They are after Derby figures, copied circa 1760 from Meissen figures modeled by Kaendler and Eberlein, circa 1740. The figures were supposedly inspired by a real incident. Count Heinrich von Bruhl (1700–1763) was Prime Minister of Saxony and Director of Meissen from 1735. A profligate dandy, he offered his tailor a reward of his choosing for meeting a deadline. The tailor asked to attend a court banquet. This request was considered ridiculous, so instead porcelain forms of the tailor and his wife were placed as table decorations on the count's banquet table. "Welsh" in the figure's title results from the incorrect translation of Meissen's title of the tailor, "Ein Schneider welcher auf einem Ziegenbock reutet" (a tailor who rides a goat). All recorded examples are made without bocages.

Figure 152.1. The Welsh Tailor and his wife, a pair. Probably made by "Sherratt". H: 6.4" (L), 6.5" (R). The subject and the figures' bases are both unusual for "Sherratt". The flowers on the bases and other features support attribution. Price B.

Figure 152.2. The Welsh Tailor and his wife, reverse of previous pair. The border of stiff leaves on the front of each base does not extend to the back.

Figure 152.3. The Welsh Tailor's wife. Possibly made by "Sherratt". H: ~6.5". "Sherratt" made this subject on this base, and examples are recorded with characteristic flowers on their bases. The dress pattern here is very suggestive of "Sherratt". Price A.

Figure 152.4. The Welsh Tailor and his wife, a pair. H: ~6". The figure of the wife sometimes does not have a small goat on the base. Price B. *John Howard; www.antiquepottery.co.uk.*

Figure 152.5. The Welsh Tailor and his wife, a pair. H: ~6". Price B. *Andrew Dando Antiques.*

Figure 152.6. The Welsh Tailor and his wife, a pair. H: ~6". Price B. *Andrew Dando Antiques.*

Figure 152.7. The Welsh Tailor and his wife, reverse of previous pair. *Andrew Dando Antiques.*

Figure 152.8. The Welsh Tailor's wife. H: ~6". Price A.

Figure 152.9. The Welsh Tailor. H: ~6". The pair of scissors customarily on his coat is absent. Price A.

Figure 152.10. The Welsh Tailor and his wife, a pair. Possibly made by Enoch Wood. H: ~5.3". The bases, which are lower than those on previous examples, are decorated and made in the style of Enoch Wood. Price B.

Figure 152.11. The Welsh Tailor's wife. H: ~5.3". Price A.

Figure 152.12. The Welsh Tailor's wife. Attributed to Leather Leaf Group. H: ~6". Characteristic Leather Leaf Group flowers are on the base. Price A.

153. The Elements

The four classical elements, water, fire, earth, and air, are portrayed in figural form with their attributes. Water holds fish, fire holds a flaming torch, earth has a spade, and air holds a bird. The illustrations in Cesare Ripa's *Iconologia* established these personifications. Today, figures emblematic of the Four Elements seldom occur in sets, but patient collectors can assemble four matching figures into a set. For other figures of a classically attired lady holding a bird, see figures of Venus.

Figure 153.1. *Air.* Lady holding a bird, emblematic of air. Attributed to Ralph Wood. H: ~8". This figure, like its two companions that follow, is titled and decorated in a typical Ralph Wood manner. Price A.

Figure 153.2. *Fire*. Man blowing onto a flaming torch, emblematic of fire. Attributed to Ralph Wood. H: ~8". Price A.

Figure 153.3. *Water.* Lady standing beside flowing water, emblematic of water. Attributed to Ralph Wood. H: 7.9". Price A. *Elinor Penna*.

Figure 153.4. Two figures, each standing beside flowing water, emblematic of water. Attributed to Ralph Wood (L); probably made by Dudson (R). H: 7.9". The figures are from the same molds, which Dudson probably acquired when Ralph Wood's manufactory closed. Price A each. *Elinor Penna.*

Figure 153.5. The bases of the previous figures of water. Although the figures are from the same mold forms, the bases are finished quite differently. The figure on the left has a typical Ralph Wood base, while the figure on the right has a typical Dudson base. *Elinor Penna.*

Figure 153.6. *Earth.* Man holding a spade, emblematic of earth. Probably made by Dudson. H: ~7.8". Price A. *Andrew Dando Antiques.*

Figure 153.7. *Fire.* Man blowing, emblematic of fire. Probably made by Dudson. H: 7.8". A flaming torch was in his lower hand, now lost. Price A. *Elinor Penna.*

Figure 153.8. *Air.* Lady holding a bird, emblematic of air. Probably made by Dudson. H: 8". Price A. *Elinor Penna.*

Figure 153.9. Lady standing beside flowing water, emblematic of water; man holding a spade, emblematic of earth. A pair. H: 8". From the Ralph Wood molds also used by Dudson but with adaptations (figs. 153.4, 153.6). She now holds a jug, and he holds a pot. Price A. *Aurea Carter Antiques.*

Figure 153.10. Lady holding fish and standing beside water, emblematic of water. H: 8.5". The painter's mark of William Absolon of Yarmouth is beneath. Price A. *Aurea Carter Antiques.*

Figure 153.11. Base of the previous figure emblematic of water, with "Absolon Yarm" painted beneath. For that reason, this figure predates 1815. The following two figures have bases formed in the same manner. *Aurea Carter Antiques.*

Figure 153.12. Man holding a spade, emblematic of earth. H: 8.5". Companion to the previous and following figures and probably also painted by William Absolon. Price A. *Brighton and Hove Museums.*

Figure 153.13. Lady holding a bird, emblematic of air. H: ~8.5". Faces representing the wind are at her feet. Companion to the previous two figures and from the same sources. Price A.

Figure 153.14. *WATER*. Lady holding fish in her apron; with bocage. Emblematic of water. Impressed "I. DALE BURSLEM". H: 6.4". Price B.

Figure 153.15. *WATER*. Lady holding fish in her apron; with bocage. Emblematic of water. Impressed "I. DALE BURSLEM". H: 6.4". Like the previous Dale figure but without a plume on the hat. Price B. © *Victoria and Albert Museum, London.*

Figure 153.16. *EARTH*. Man holding a pot and a spade; with bocage. Emblematic of earth. Impressed "I. DALE BURSLEM". H: ~6.5". The grape sprig on the base is exclusive to Dale. Price B.

Figure 153.17. *EARTH*. Man holding a pot and a spade; with bocage. Emblematic of earth. Impressed "I. DALE BURSLEM". H: ~6.5". Like the previous figure but with a characteristic Dale floral sprig on the base. Price B.

Figure 153.18. *AIR*. Lady holding a bird; with bocage. Emblematic of air. Impressed "I. DALE BURSLEM". H: ~6.5". The bocage flowers have eight petals and are of a form believed to be exclusive to Dale. Price B.

Figure 153.19. *FIRE*. Man holding a magnifier and torch; with bocage. Emblematic of fire. Impressed "I. DALE BURSLEM". H: ~6.5". The eight-petalled bocage flowers and the sprig on the base are characteristic Dale features. Price A.

Figure 153.20. *FIRE*. Man emblematic of fire. Impressed "I. DALE BURSLEM". H: 6.5". With losses. Like the previous figure but painted quite differently. Price A. © *Victoria and Albert Museum, London*.

Figure 153.21. *EARTH, AIR, FIRE, WATER*. A set of figures emblematic of the elements; with bocages. All impressed "I. DALE BURSLEM". H: ~7". Price C.

Figure 153.22. *AIR, EARTH*. Lady holding a bird, man holding a flower pot and spade; with bocages. A pair of figures emblematic of air and earth. Attributed to "Sherratt". H: ~7". The flower on her hat is specific to "Sherratt". The dress pattern and bocage flowers are consistent with the attribution. Price B. *John Howard; www.antiquepottery.co.uk.*

Figure 153.23. *WATER*. Lady with fish in her apron; with bocage. Emblematic of water. Attributed to "Sherratt". H: ~7". Companion model to the previous pair of figures. The small flowers on her hat are specific to "Sherratt" and the cockade is a "Sherratt" feature. Price A.

Figure 153.24. *AIR*. Lady holding a bird; with bocage. Emblematic of air. Attributed to "Sherratt". H: ~7". Like the previous figure emblematic of air (fig. 153.22) but with a typical "Sherratt" oak-leaf bocage. Price A.

Figure 153.25. *WATER, EARTH*. Lady with fish in her apron, man holding a flower pot and spade; with bocages. A pair of figures emblematic of water and earth. Attributed to "Sherratt". H: 7". Price B.

Figure 153.26. *EARTH*. Man holding a flower pot and spade; with bocage. Emblematic of earth. Attributed to "Sherratt". H: ~7". The combination of these flowers with anthemion leaves (always arranged in twos on "Sherratt" bocages) supports the attribution. Price A.

Figure 153.27. *FIRE*. Man holding a magnifier and torch; with bocage. Emblematic of fire. Attributed to "Sherratt". H: ~6.3". This example of FIRE is significantly smaller than other "Sherratt" elements, possibly due to excessive shrinkage in firing. Price A.

Figure 153.28. *AIR*. Lady with a bird; with bocage. Emblematic of air. Probably made by "Sherratt". H: 7". The clusters of five-petalled bocage flowers are very suggestive of "Sherratt," as is the cockade on her hat. Price A. *Peter Flemans*.

Figure 153.29. *FIRE*. Man holding magnifier and torch; with bocage. Emblematic of fire. Probably made by "Sherratt". H: 7". The five-petalled bocage flowers clustered in threes and the turquoise palette suggest the attribution. Price A. *Peter Flemans*.

Figure 153.30. Lady holding a bird; with bocage. Emblematic of air. H: 7.1". Indistinguishable in form from the following marked Walton figure and possibly, but not necessarily, made by Walton. Price A. *Elinor Penna*.

Figure 153.31. Lady holding a bird, emblematic of air, reverse of previous figure. *Elinor Penna*.

Figure 153.32. Lady holding a bird; with bocage. Emblematic of air. Marked "WALTON". H: 7". Price A. *John Howard; www.antiquepottery.co.uk.*

Figure 153.33. Lady with fish in her apron; with bocage. Emblematic of water. Marked "WALTON". H: ~7". Price A.

Figure 153.34. Man holding a magnifier and torch; with bocage. Emblematic of fire. Marked "WALTON". H: 6.8". Price A.

Figure 153.35. Man holding a flower pot and spade; with bocage. Emblematic of earth. Marked "WALTON". H: ~6.9". The round object on the ground (perhaps a vegetable) is not present on stylistically similar Walton figures of gardeners. Price A.

Figure 153.37. *AIR, FIRE*. Lady holding a bird, man holding a torch and magnifier; with bocages. A pair of figures emblematic of air and fire. Impressed "SALT". H: 7". Price B. *John Howard; www.antiquepottery.co.uk.*

Figure 153.36. Figures emblematic of earth, air, fire, and water; with bocages. All marked "WALTON". H: ~7". The bases on Walton elements do not match, suggesting that the figures were intended to stand alone. Price C.

Figure 153.38. Lady holding a bird; with bocage. Emblematic of air. Impressed "SALT". H: 7.1". Like the previous Salt AIR but untitled. Price A.

Figure 153.39. *AIR*. Lady holding a bird; with bocage. Emblematic of air. Impressed "SALT". H: ~7". Note that "Selina" is painted on the front of her dress. Price A.

Figure 153.40. WATER. Lady with fish in her apron; with bocage. Emblematic of water. Impressed "SALT". H: ~7". Price A. *www.madelena.com*.

Figure 153.41. *EARTH*. Man holding a flower pot and spade; with bocage. Emblematic of earth. Impressed "SALT". H: ~7". Some bocage restoration. Price A.

Figure 153.42. *FIRE, WATER, EARTH, AIR*. Figures emblematic of the four elements; with bocages. All impressed "SALT". H: ~7". The bases of Salt elements, like those made by Walton, do not match, and perhaps the figures were not intended for purchase as a set. Price C.

Figure 153.43. *WATER*. Lady with fish in her apron; with bocage. Emblematic of water. H: ~7". Indistinguishable from the marked Salt *WATER* and possibly, but not necessarily, made by Salt. Price A.

Figure 153.44. Man holding a magnifier and torch; with bocage. Emblematic of fire. H: ~7". Like the marked Salt *FIRE*, but other potters made figures indistinguishable from Salt's. Price A.

Figure 153.45. *FIRE*. Man holding a magnifier and torch; with bocage. Emblematic of fire. H: ~7". Like the marked Salt *FIRE* but with blue carnations. Blue flowers have not been recorded on a marked Salt figure. Price A. *Collection of Michael J. Smith*.

Figure 153.46. *EARTH*. Man holding a flower pot and spade; with bocage. Emblematic of earth. H: ~7". In the style of marked Salt figures. Price A.

Figure 153.47. Figures emblematic of Fire. Marked "I. DALE BURSLEM" (L), "WALTON" (center), "SALT" (R). H: 7". The figures are remarkably similar. Some bocage restoration. Price A each.

Figure 153.48. *WATER, FIRE*. Lady with fish in her apron, man holding a magnifier and torch; with bocages. An assembled pair of figures emblematic of Water and Fire. Probably attributable to the Box Title Group. H: ~7". Restored bocages. The green-turquoise enameling on the base of Fire strongly suggests a Box Title Group attribution. Price A.

Figure 153.49. *AIR, EARTH*. Lady holding a bird, man holding a flower pot and spade; with bocages. A pair of figures emblematic of air and earth. Probably attributable to Box Title Group. H: ~7". The boxed titles coupled with the green-turquoise painting of his base suggest the attribution. Restoration to bocages. Price A.

Figure 153.50. *EARTH*. Man holding a flower pot and spade; with bocage. Emblematic of earth. Probably attributable to Box Title Group. H: 6.6". On the same base as the previous example of Earth but in unrestored condition. Price A. *Peter Flemans*.

Figure 153.51. Lady with fish in her apron, emblematic of water. Made without bocage. H: 6.4". Price A. *www.madelena.com*.

Figure 153.52. Lady with fish in her apron, emblematic of water. Possibly made by Enoch Wood. H: 6.5". Made without bocage. Price A. *Aurea Carter Antiques*.

Figure 153.53. Man holding a magnifier and torch, emblematic of fire. Possibly made by Enoch Wood. H: ~6.7". Made without bocage. Price A. *Andrew Dando Antiques*.

Figure 153.54. Man holding a magnifier and torch, emblematic of fire. Possibly made by Enoch Wood. H: ~6.7". Flames are painted on the clothing, as sometimes occurs on figures emblematic of fire. Made without bocage. Price A. *Andrew Dando Antiques.*

Figure 153.55. Man holding a flower pot and spade, emblematic of earth. Possibly made by Enoch Wood. Made without bocage. H: ~6.7". Price A.

Figure 153.56. Man holding a magnifier and torch; with bocage. Emblematic of fire. Probably made by Enoch Wood. H: ~7". The base and bocage are in the style of Enoch Wood, and the figure is a companion to the following figures emblematic of air, water, and earth. Price A. *Andrew Dando Antiques.*

Figure 153.57. Lady holding a bird; with bocage. Emblematic of air. Probably made by Enoch Wood. H: ~7". Price A.

Figure 153.58. Lady with fish in her apron; with bocage. Emblematic of water. Possibly made by Enoch Wood. H: ~7". The bocage is restored, but the base is in the style of Enoch Wood. Price A.

Figure 153.59. Man holding a flower pot and spade handle (spade lost); with bocage. Emblematic of earth. Probably made by Enoch Wood. H: 7". Price A. *William Brook.*

Figure 153.60. Figures emblematic of water, fire, air, and earth; with bocages. H: ~7". The bocages (largely restored) and the bases are in the style of Enoch Wood. Price B.

Figure 153.61. *AIR*. Lady holding a bird; with bocage. Emblematic of air. Attributed to Blue Group. H: ~6.8". Price A.

Figure 153.62. *WATER*. Lady with fish in her apron; with bocage. Emblematic of water. Attributed to Blue Group. H: ~6.8". The bocage is as on the previous figure emblematic of air, but it is painted differently. Price A.

Figure 153.63. *EARTH*. Man holding a flower pot and spade; with bocage. Emblematic of earth. Attributed to Blue Group. H: 6.7". Left side of the bocage restored. Price A.

154. The Quarters of the Globe

In the eighteenth century, porcelain factories introduced allegorical representations of the four quarters of the globe. The porcelain figures portray Asia, Africa, Europe, and America and are stylistically similar to the earthenware personifications shown here. These are among the rarest of earthenware figures and are recorded only from these examples.

Figure 154.1. *EUROP*. Europe portrayed as a regally clad girl, with crown, orb, and scepter, a horse at her side, a skull and crossbones and other objects at her feet; with bocage. H: 6". Price B.

Figure 154.2. *EUROP.* Reverse of previous figure. Part of the bocage was lost in the biscuit firing. The stump was then glazed and painted.

Figure 154.3. *EUROP.* Europe portrayed as a regally clad girl, with crown, orb, and scepter, a horse at her side, a skull and crossbones and other objects at her feet; with bocage. H: 6". Like the previous figure but with a different bocage. Both bocages are consistent with an Enoch Wood attribution. Price B. *Bearnes Hampton & Littlewood.*

Figure 154.4. *AFRICA*. Africa portrayed as an African girl crowned with an elephant headdress and holding a cornucopia, a lion beside her. H: 6.2". Bocage lost. Companion to the previous *EUROP* figures and the following *ASIA*. Price A. *Bearnes Hampton & Littlewood.*

Figure 154.5. *ASIA*. Asia portrayed as a girl holding a quiver with a crocodile at her feet. H: 6". The quiver and crocodile are traditionally associated with America and occur on porcelain figures representing America. Companion to previous figures of *EUROP* and *AFRICA*. Losses and restored bocage. Price A. *Bearnes Hampton & Littlewood.*

Figure 154.6. A regally clad girl holding an incense burner, a snake-entwined camel beside her; with bocage. Emblematic of Asia. Attributed to Blue Group. H: ~6". Left side of bocage and her right arm restored. Price A.

Figure 154.7. A girl crowned with an elephant headdress and holding a cornucopia, a lion beside her; with bocage. Emblematic of Africa. Attributed to Blue Group. H: ~6". Bocage largely restored. Price A.

155. The Seasons

From Roman times, artists have paid tribute to the seasons with their works. In the classical tradition, the seasons were represented by Flora or Venus (spring), Ceres (summer), Bacchus (autumn), and Vulcan or Boreas (winter). In the eighteenth century, the seasons were particularly pertinent because of James Thomson's *Seasons*, four poems each named for a season and first published as a complete edition in 1730. Frequently embellished with elegant engravings, the poems became perennial favorites.

Figure 155.1. *Autumn, Winter.* Reverse-painted print applied to glass, circa 1800. This print is the design source for some of the figures that follow. *Elinor Penna.*

Figure 155.2. *Spring, Summer*. Reverse-painted print applied to glass, circa 1800. This print is the design source for some of the figures that follow.

Figure 155.3. Lady in a fur coat with a child; with bocage. Emblematic of winter. Impressed "WALTON". H: 9". No other marked Walton example of this figure is recorded. Makes a set with the following three figures. Price E, set.

Figure 155.4. Lady holding grapes and a basket of produce, with a child; with bocage. Emblematic of autumn. Impressed "WALTON". H: 9". A similar marked figure is in the *Brighton and Hove Museums*. With the previous and following two figures, it makes a full set. Price E, set.

Figure 155.5. Lady holding a sickle, child with wheat; with bocage. Emblematic of summer. Impressed "WALTON". H: 9". No other marked Walton example of this figure is recorded. The child is restored. With the previous and following figures, it makes a full set. Price E, set.

Figure 155.6. Lady holding a flower with child holding a bird's nest; with bocage. Emblematic of spring. Impressed "WALTON". H: 9". With the previous three figures, it makes a full set. Price E, set.

Figure 155.7. Lady holding a flower with child holding a bird's nest; with scroll. Emblematic of spring. Impressed "WALTON". H: 8.8". Like the previous figure, these two being the only known marked Walton examples. The leafy scroll occurs on other figures representing seasons but on no other marked Walton figures. Price B.

Figure 155.8. Lady with a child holding a bird's nest; with scroll. Emblematic of spring. H: 8.6". Like the previous Walton figure and having the same scroll behind but lacking features for attribution. A companion to the following two figures. Price B. *Elinor Penna.*

Figure 155.9. Lady holding a flower and a basket of flowers or produce, with a child; with scroll. Emblematic of autumn. H: 9". A companion to the previous and following figures. Price B. *Elinor Penna.*

Figure 155.10. Lady in a fur coat with a child; with scroll. Emblematic of winter. H: 9.2". Companion to the previous two figures and, like them, uses the same figure molds as the previous marked Walton figures. Price B. *The William Herbert and Nancy Hunt Collection.*

Figure 155.11. Lady in a fur coat with a child; with scroll. Emblematic of winter. H: 8.4". Companion to the following two figures. Price B.

Figure 155.12. Lady holding a flower with a child holding a bird's nest; with scroll. Emblematic of spring. H: 8.6". Differs from similar portrayals of spring in that the child is placed to the left rather than the right. Companion to the previous and following figures. Price B. *Elinor Penna*.

Figure 155.13. Lady holding a sickle with a child holding wheat; with scroll. Emblematic of summer. H: ~8.7". Companion to the previous two figures. Price B.

Figure 155.14. Lady holding a sickle with a child holding wheat; with scroll. Emblematic of summer. H: 9". Price B. *Elinor Penna*.

Figure 155.15. Lady holding wheat with a child holding wheat; with scroll. Emblematic of summer. H: 9.5". The figures are from the molds used for the Walton figure of summer, but the base is different, and the group lacks features to support attribution. On the same base as the following figure of spring but painted differently. Price B. *Elinor Penna*.

Figure 155.16. Lady holding a flower with a child holding a bird's nest; with scroll. Emblematic of spring. H: 9". On the same base as the previous figure of summer. Price B. *Elinor Penna*.

Figure 155.17. Lady in fur coat with a child; with scroll. Emblematic of winter. H: 9". Scrolls in lieu of bocages are recorded only on figures emblematic of the seasons. Price B. *Elinor Penna*.

Figure 155.18. Lady holding a flower and a basket of flowers or produce, with a child; with scroll. Emblematic of autumn. H: 9". Probably a companion to the previous figure. Price B. *Elinor Penna*.

Figure 155.19. Lady holding a flower with a child holding a bird's nest; with bocage. Emblematic of spring. H: ~9.2". Companion subject to following figure. Price B.

Figure 155.20. Lady holding an unidentified object and a basket of produce, with a child. Emblematic of autumn. H: 9.5", L: 7.5". Bocage lost. A companion subject to the previous example. Price A. *Image courtesy of The Potteries Museum & Art Gallery, Stoke-on-Trent, UK.*

Figure 155.21. Lady, emblematic of autumn, reverse of previous figure. The vestiges of the bocage indicate that the bocage fronds were unlike those on figure 155.19, which is on the same base. *Image courtesy of The Potteries Museum & Art Gallery, Stoke-on-Trent, UK.*

Figure 155.22. *WINTER* (impressed beneath). Girl swathed in a cloak. Impressed "NEALE & Co". H: 5.5". Neale and Neale-type figures of the seasons are frequently titled beneath. Price B. *Image courtesy of The Potteries Museum & Art Gallery, Stoke-on-Trent, UK.*

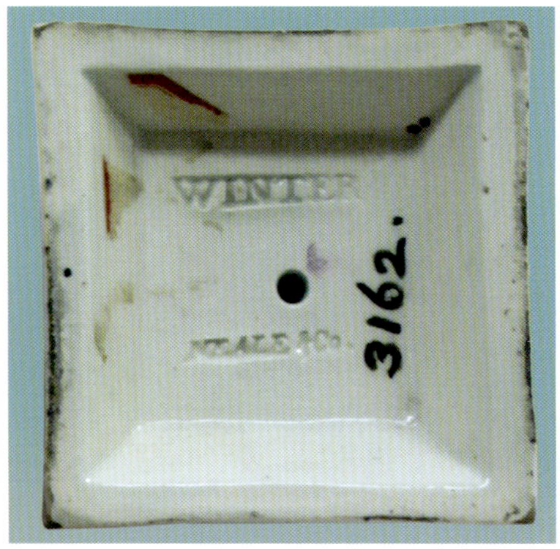

Figure 155.23. Base of previous figure of winter showing the impressed title and the "NEALE & Co" mark. *Image courtesy of The Potteries Museum & Art Gallery, Stoke-on-Trent, UK.*

Figure 155.24. *SUMMER* (impressed beneath). Boy with wheat. Impressed "NEALE & Co". H: 5.4". James Neale was active as a sole proprietor from 1778 to 1783 and withdrew from manufacturing in 1789, so his marked figures can be placed within this time frame. Price B. *Image courtesy of The Potteries Museum & Art Gallery, Stoke-on-Trent, UK.*

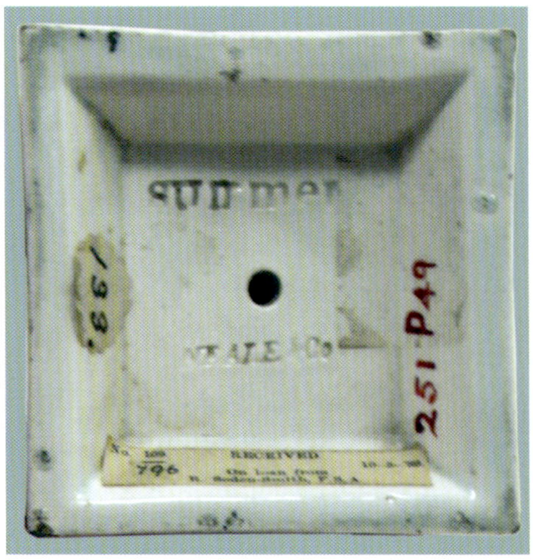

Figure 155.25. Base of previous figure of *SUMMER* showing the title and maker's mark. Neale made these figures of the seasons in both porcelain and earthenware. *Image courtesy of The Potteries Museum & Art Gallery, Stoke-on-Trent, UK.*

Figure 155.26. *SPRING* (illegibly impressed beneath). Girl with flowers. Impressed "NEALE & Co". H: 5.5". Price B. © *Victoria and Albert Museum, London*.

Figure 155.27. *SPRING* (girl with flowers), *AUTUMN* (girl with grapes), *WINTER* (girl in cloak), titles impressed beneath. Probably made by Neale & Co. H: ~5.5". Unmarked but indistinguishable from marked Neale examples and almost certainly made by Neale or his successor Robert Wilson. Price B. *Angus Northeast*.

Figure 155.28. Bases of previous figures of *SPRING, AUTUMN*, and *WINTER*. Such bases are recorded on other Neale figures. However, the bases are formed differently from those of the previous marked Neale examples and from those on subsequent marked Wilson examples. *Angus Northeast*.

Figure 155.29. *SPRING* (girl with flowers), *SUMMER* (boy with wheat), *AUTUMN* (girl with grapes), *WINTER* (girl in cloak), titles impressed beneath. Probably made by Neale & Co. H: 5.5". Marked Neale figures of summer often have a black dot on the hat, as seen here. Price C. *Nick Burton*.

Figure 155.30. *SPRING* (girl with flowers), *SUMMER* (boy with wheat), *AUTUMN* (girl with grapes), *WINTER* (girl in cloak), titles impressed beneath. Impressed with "G" and a crown, the mark of Robert Wilson. H: 5.5". Wilson was Neale's partner, and he bought out Neale in 1789 and continued using the same molds. Price C.

Figure 155.31. Bases of previous figures of *SPRING, SUMMER, AUTUMN, WINTER*, showing the titles and Wilson's mark. The bases are indistinguishable from those on marked Neale figures.

Figure 155.32. *SUMMER* (boy with wheat), *AUTUMN* (girl with grapes), titles impressed beneath. Impressed with "G" and a crown, the mark of Robert Wilson. H: 5.5". Like previous Wilson examples with bases formed in the same way, but the figures are not as well painted. Price A.

Figure 155.33. *SPRING* (impressed beneath). Classical youth with flowers. Attributed to Neale & Co/Wilson. H: 5.6". This pot bank made seasons in two styles: contemporary (see figures above) and classical. The classical figure of autumn follows. Price A. *Elinor Penna*.

Figure 155.34. Base of the previous figure of *SPRING*, showing the impressed title. The base is finished in a manner consistent with a Neale/Wilson attribution. *Elinor Penna*.

Figure 155.35. Classical youth holding flowers and grapes, emblematic of autumn. Attributed to Neale & Co/Wilson. H: 5.4". Companion to the previous figure of spring. The interiors of both bases are finished in the same manner. Price A. *Elinor Penna*.

Figure 155.36. Classical youth holding grapes, emblematic of autumn. H: 5.4". The rounded internal corners of the base have been scored with a knife, as on some Neale/Wilson figures. Price A. *Elinor Penna*.

Figure 155.37. Boy holding wheat, emblematic of summer. H: 5.5". Figures of Apollo and Ceres also occur on this base. Price A. *Elinor Penna*.

Figure 155.38. Figure wrapped in a cloak, emblematic of winter. H: 5.7". On the same base as the previous and following figures, but the previous figure is from a set of seasons in contemporary attire, while the following figure is from a classically styled set. Price A. *Elinor Penna*.

Figure 155.39. Figure holding a cornucopia of flowers, emblematic of spring. H: 5.7". Price A. *Elinor Penna*.

Figure 155.40. Figure wearing a cloak, emblematic of winter. H: 5.1". Companion to the following figure of autumn. Price A. *Elinor Penna*.

Figure 155.41. Lady holding a basket, probably emblematic of autumn. H: 5.5". Probably after the Neale-type figure of autumn. Companion to the previous figure of winter. Price A. *Elinor Penna*.

Figure 155.42. *SUMMER*. Lady holding a cornucopia. Impressed "DIXON, AUSTIN, & Co". H: 9.3". Forms a set with the following three figures. Price D, set.

Figure 155.43. *SPRING*. Lady alongside a cornucopia. Impressed "DIXON, AUSTIN, & Co". H: 8.6". Forms a set with the previous figure and following two figures. Price D, set.

Figure 155.44. *AUTUMN*. Lady with sickle and wheat. Impressed "DIXON, AUSTIN, & Co". H: 8.7". Forms a set with the following figure and previous two figures. Note autumn carries wheat, usually carried by summer in differently styled figures by other pot banks. Price D, set.

Figure 155.45. *WINTER*. Figure swathed in a cloak. Impressed "DIXON, AUSTIN, & Co". H: 9.4". Forms a set with the previous three figures. Price D, set.

Figure 155.46. Base of previous figure of *WINTER*. All figures in the set are marked thus. This mark was used from December 1818 to December 1839.

Figure 155.47. Watch stand flanked by figures of autumn and summer. Impressed "DIXON, AUSTIN, & Co". H: 11". The only recorded Dixon and Austin watch stand with these large figures. Usually, small nondescript classical figures flank the clock (fig. 198.25). Price C. *Jonathan Horne.*

Figure 155.48. *SPRING* (lady beside cornucopia), *SUMMER* (lady holding cornucopia), *AUTUMN* (lady with sickle and wheat), *WINTER* (figure swathed in cloak). All impressed "DIXON, AUSTIN, & Co". H: 8.6"–9.4". Like the previous set, these examples are decorated lavishly with pink luster. Price D, set. *Collection of Michael J. Smith*.

Figure 155.49. *SUMMER* (lady holding cornucopia), *SPRING* (lady beside cornucopia). H: 9.4" (L), 8.9" (R). Forms a set with the following two figures. Price D, set. *Brighton and Hove Museums*.

Figure 155.50. *WINTER* (figure swathed in cloak), *AUTUMN* (lady with wheat and sickle). H: 9.3" (L), 8.9" (R). Forms a set with the previous two figures. Price D, set. *Brighton and Hove Museums*.

Figure 155.51. Lady with sickle and wheat, emblematic of autumn. H: 8.2". In the same style as the Dixon, Austin & Co. *AUTUMN* in figures 155.44 and 155.48. Price A. *Image courtesy of The Potteries Museum & Art Gallery, Stoke-on-Trent, UK.*

Figure 155.52. Lady holding a cornucopia, emblematic of summer. H: 8.7". In the style of the Dixon, Austin & Co. *SUMMER* in figures 155.42 and 155.48. Price A. *Michael Goodacre*.

Figure 155.53. Figure wrapped in a cloak, emblematic of winter. H: 8.3".Companion to the following figure. Price A. *Elinor Penna*.

Figure 155.54. Figure with cornucopia, emblematic of spring. H: 8.3". Companion to the previous and following figures, all styled after the Dixon, Austin & Co. figures. Price A. *Elinor Penna*.

Figure 155.55. Figure with cloak, emblematic of winter; figure with cornucopia, emblematic of summer. H: 8.5". Companion subjects to the previous figure. Price A. *Skinner, Inc.; www.skinnerinc.com.*

Figure 155.56. Figure wrapped in a cloak, emblematic of winter. H: 8.2". Price A. *Elinor Penna*.

Figure 155.57. Lady holding a floral garland, emblematic of spring. H: 5.5". Made without bocage. Impressed "30" beneath, suggesting an Enoch Wood origin. Makes a set with figures 155.59, 155.60, and 155.61. Price A. *Michael Goodacre*.

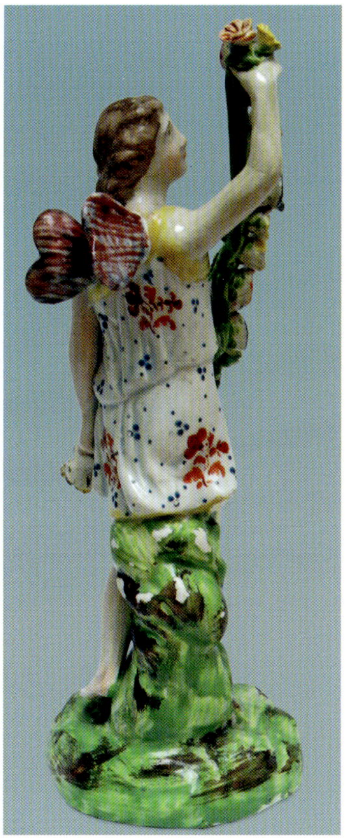

Figure 155.58. Lady emblematic of spring, reverse of previous figure. *Michael Goodacre.*

Figure 155.59. Lady holding a sickle, emblematic of summer. H: ~5.3". Made without bocage. Makes a set with figures 155.57, 155.60, and 155.61. A similar figure in the Fitzwilliam Museum (c.935.1928) is mounted atop a square green base, in the manner of figures 155.101–104. Price A.

Figure 155.60. Figure wrapped in a cloak, emblematic of winter. H: ~5.3". Made without bocage. Makes a set with figures 155.57, 155.59, and 155.61. This figure model was reproduced circa 1900. Price A.

Figure 155.61. Man (possibly Bacchus) with grapes in his hair and drinking from a goblet, emblematic of autumn. H: ~5.3". Made without bocage. Makes a set with figures 155.57, 155.59, and 155.60. A similar example in the Fitzwilliam Museum (c.934.1928) is mounted atop a square green base, in the manner of figures 155.101–104. Price A.

Figure 155.62. Man (possibly Bacchus) with grapes in his hair and drinking from a goblet; with bocage. Emblematic of autumn. H: ~6.5". Like the previous figure but more fully clothed and made with a bocage. Price A.

Figure 155.63. Three ladies emblematic of spring, summer, and winter. H: 7". No other examples of these figures are recorded. Price B. *Byrne's Auctioneers, Chester.*

Figure 155.64. Man holding grapes and a goblet, emblematic of autumn; lady holding wheat and a sickle, emblematic of summer. Made by Peter and Francis Warburton. H: 7". Both impressed "P & F WARBURTON". The bodies are creamware. Price B. *Image courtesy of The Potteries Museum & Art Gallery, Stoke-on-Trent, UK.*

Figure 155.65. The Warburton mark on the reverse of the previous figure emblematic of autumn. The Warburtons operated in Cobridge from 1795 to 1802. No enamel-painted figures are documented, but these unpainted figures evidence that figures of this form were produced before 1803. *Image courtesy of The Potteries Museum & Art Gallery, Stoke-on-Trent, UK.*

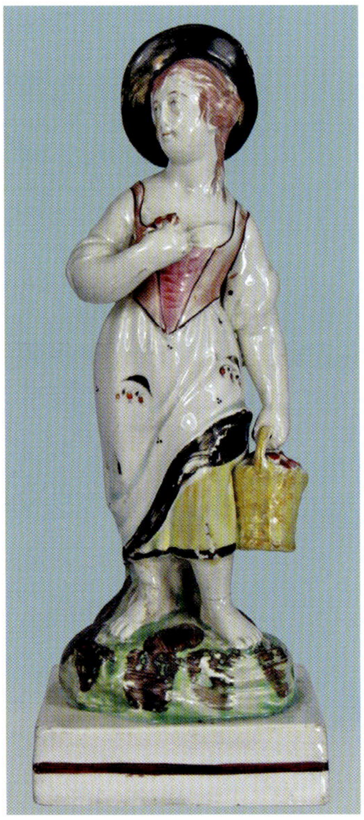

Figure 155.66. Lady holding a flower and a basket, emblematic of spring. Possibly made by Enoch Wood. H: 7.5". Made without bocage. Companion model to the following figures of the seasons. Price A.

Figure 155.67. Lady holding wheat and a sickle, emblematic of summer. Possibly made by Enoch Wood. H: 7.5". Made without bocage. Companion model to the previous figure of spring and the following figures of autumn and winter. Price A.

Figure 155.68. Man holding grapes and a goblet, emblematic of autumn. Possibly made by Enoch Wood. H: 7.5". Made without bocage. Companion model to the previous figures of spring and summer and the next figure of winter. Price A.

Figure 155.69. Man holding grapes and a goblet, emblematic of autumn. Possibly made by Enoch Wood. Painted "Absolon yarm" beneath. H: ~7.5". Made without bocage. From the same molds as the previous figure of autumn, but here the mound is exactly as wide as the square base. Price A.

Figure 155.70. Autumn, base of previous figure showing the painter's mark used by William Absolon of Yarmouth between 1784 and 1815. The base is fashioned like other Enoch Wood bases.

Figure 155.71. Two figures of a man wearing cloak and skates, emblematic of winter. Possibly made by Enoch Wood. H: 7.6" (L), 7.4" (R). Made without bocage. The two figures are from different molds and may or may not originate from the same pot bank. On one the mound overhangs the base. The bases are formed identically from beneath. Price A each.

Figure 155.72. Four figures emblematic of autumn, summer, winter, and spring. Possibly made by Enoch Wood. H: 7.5"–7.7". Made without bocages. Only winter stands on a drum-shaped mound. These figure models can differ markedly in size, and more than one pot bank may have made them. Price B.

Figure 155.73. Reverse of previous set emblematic of autumn, summer, winter, and spring.

Figure 155.74. Man wearing cloak and skates, emblematic of winter. H: 7.5". Painted in an unusual manner. Price A. *Andrew Dando Antiques.*

Figure 155.75 Man wearing cloak and skates, emblematic of winter. H: ~8". Price A. *Andrew Dando Antiques.*

Figure 155.76. Man wearing cloak and skates; with scroll. Emblematic of winter. H: 7". The base differs from that of other similar examples of winter. Price A. *Phil Masters Antiques, Leek.*

Figure 155.77. Man wearing cloak and skates; with bocage. Emblematic of winter. Possibly made by Enoch Wood. H: ~7.7". Bocage restored. This figure is on a taller mound than used for similar figures atop square bases (see fig. 155.71). Price A.

Figure 155.78. Man holding grapes and a goblet; with bocage. Emblematic of autumn. Possibly made by Enoch Wood. H: ~7". Bocage restored. This figure also occurs impressed "12" beneath. Price A.

Figure 155.79. Figures emblematic of autumn and winter. H: ~7.7" max. These figures, previously illustrated, show considerable variation in size when placed side by side. Such figures emblematic of the seasons appear to have been made in sets of two sizes. Price A.

Figure 155.80. Lady holding wheat and a sickle; with bocage. Emblematic of summer. Possibly made by Enoch Wood. H: ~7.5". Bocage restored. The base is in the style of Enoch Wood. Price A.

Figure 155.81. Lady holding wheat and a sickle; with bocage. Emblematic of summer. Probably made by Enoch Wood. H: 7.1". The base is in the style of Enoch Wood, and the bocage is typical. Price A. *Michael Goodacre*.

Figure 155.82. Lady holding wheat and a sickle, with spill vase. Emblematic of summer. Possibly made by Enoch Wood. H: 7.5". The figure's form and the yellow and brown acorns suggest an Enoch Wood attribution. The bocage is suggestive but not typical and is also on figure 39.9 (Vol. 2). Price B. *Michael Goodacre*.

Figure 155.83. Lady holding a basket and a bird; with bocage. Emblematic of spring. Probably made by Enoch Wood. H: ~7.5". Some bocage restoration. Price A.

Figure 155.84. Figures emblematic of summer, autumn, spring, and winter; with bocages. Probably made by Enoch Wood. H: 7.7" max. The flower on the base of summer is specific to Enoch Wood/Wood & Caldwell. Price C, set. *Collection of Michael J. Smith.*

Figure 155.85. Lady with wheat and a sickle, emblematic of summer. H: 6.4". Made without bocage. An unusual version of this figure. Price A. *Kevin Low.*

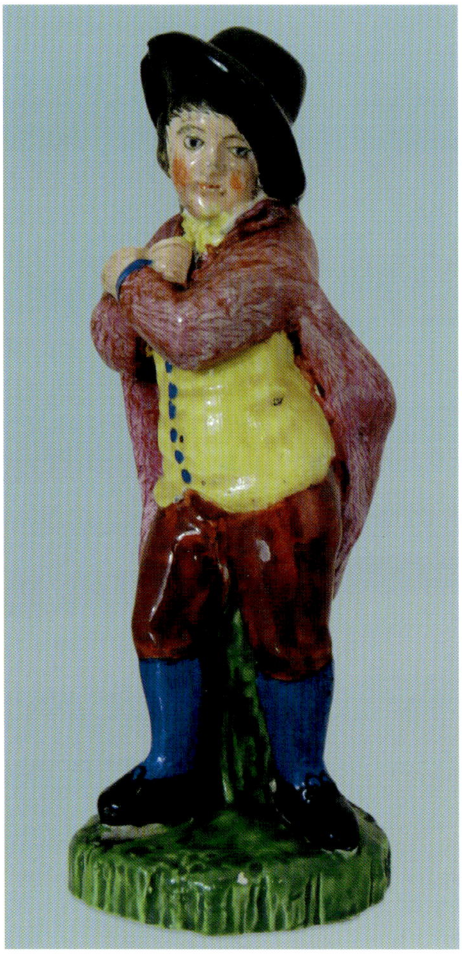

Figure 155.86. Man wearing cloak and skates. Emblematic of winter. H: 6.5". Made without bocage. Companion to the following figure. Price A. *Image courtesy of The Potteries Museum & Art Gallery, Stoke-on-Trent, UK.*

Figure 155.87. Lady emblematic of spring. H: 6.5". Objects lost from her hands. Made without bocage. Companion to the previous figure. Price A. *Image courtesy of The Potteries Museum & Art Gallery, Stoke-on-Trent, UK.*

Figure 155.88. Man holding grapes and goblet, emblematic of autumn; lady with wheat and a sickle, emblematic of summer. H: 7" each. Made without bocages. Price A each. *Bob Moores at Nestegg Antiques.*

Figure 155.89. Reverse of previous pair of figures emblematic of autumn and summer. *Bob Moores at Nestegg Antiques.*

Figure 155.90. Figures emblematic of spring, summer, autumn, and winter. Attributed to Gray Base Group. H: 7.5". Price C, set.

Figure 155.91. Lady holding basket, emblematic of spring. Attributed to Gray Base Group. H: 7.3". The figure is like spring in the previous set, but here the base is painted black, a feature found rarely on Gray Base figures. The glazes and enamels are typical of this Group. Price A.

Figure 155.92. *WINTER*. Man wearing cloak and skates. Possibly made by Ralph Wood. H: 7". This script and the line on only three sides of the base are features recorded only on Ralph Wood figures. The body is stoneware. Price A.

Figure 155.93. Man wearing cloak and skates, emblematic of winter. Possibly made by Ralph Wood. H: 7". Like the previous figure but untitled. Again, the body is stoneware. Companion to the following figures of autumn and spring. Price A.

Figure 155.94. Man holding grapes and a goblet, emblematic of autumn. Possibly made by Ralph Wood. H: 7.4". Like the previous two figures in that the body is probably stoneware and the blue line bands three sides of the base only. Companion to previous and following figures. Price A.

Figure 155.95. Lady holding a flower and a basket, emblematic of spring. Possibly made by Ralph Wood. H: 7.3". The body appears to be stoneware, and the blue line bands three sides of the base only. Companion to previous figures in the same style. Price A.

Figure 155.96. *WINTER*, spring, autumn, winter, reverse of figures 155.92–95 showing that, as occurs routinely on Ralph Wood figures, the line is not painted on the backs of the bases. A blue line is quite uncommon on earthenware figures but is recorded on a Ralph Wood *St. Peterus*.

Figure 155.97. Man wearing a cloak and skates, emblematic of winter. H: 6.9". An unusual figure. No other figures from this set are recorded. Made without bocage. Price A.

Figure 155.98. Figure emblematic of winter, previous figure from beneath.

Figure 155.99. Lady holding wheat and a sickle, emblematic of summer. Attributed to "Sherratt". H: 7.5". Made without bocage. A figure of the finest quality with multiple "Sherratt" attributes, but no other "Sherratt" seasons are recorded. Price B.

Figure 155.100. Lady emblematic of summer, reverse of previous figure. Note the painted button closure on her dress.

Figure 155.101. Lady holding wheat and a sickle, emblematic of summer. H: 6.7". Possibly attributable to Blue Group. Companion to the three figures in figures 155.102–104. Made without bocage. Price A. *Elinor Penna*.

Figure 155.102. Man, emblematic of autumn. H: ~7". Possibly attributable to Blue Group. This figure also occurs as a shepherd, attributed to the Blue Group (Vol. 1, figs. 27.147–148). It is also recorded on a base painted with only a line around it and holding large fruit. Made without bocage and companion to figures 155.101, 155.103, and 155.104. Price A.

Figure 155.103. Lady holding a flower and a basket, emblematic of spring. H: ~7". Possibly attributable to Blue Group. Forms a set with figures 155.101, 155.102, and 155.104. From the same molds as the Blue Group shepherdess (Vol. 1, figs. 27.147, 27.149). Made without bocage. Price A.

Figure 155.104. Man clutching coat, with dog, emblematic of winter. H: 6.9". Possibly attributable to Blue Group. Forms a set with the previous three figures. Made without bocage. Price A. *Andrew Dando Antiques*.

Figure 155.105. *SPRING*. Boy with fledglings in his hat; with bocage. H: ~5". Note the three-leaflet bocage fronds that occur on related figures awaiting classification. Price B.

Figure 155.106. *SPRING*. Boy with fledglings in his hat, with two sheep; with bocage. H: ~5". From the same figure molds as the previous figure but probably from a different pot bank. Companion to the following SUMMER. Price B.

Figure 155.107. *SUMMER*. Putto with two birds; with bocage. H: ~5". Companion to the previous SPRING. Note the similarity to figure 197.21. Price A.

Figure 155.108. *Autumn*. Classical figure emblematic of autumn. H: 9.8". Companion to the following figures of winter, summer and spring (figs. 155.109–111). Price A. *Image courtesy of The Potteries Museum & Art Gallery, Stoke-on-Trent, UK.*

Figure 155.109. Classical figure emblematic of winter. H: 10.1". Companion to the previous and following figures in the same style (figs. 155.108, 155.110, and 155.111). Price B. *The William Herbert and Nancy Hunt Collection.*

Figure 155.110. Classical figure emblematic of summer. H: 10". "16" is painted on the back of the plinth. Companion subject to figures 155.108, 155.109, and 155.111. Price B. *Elinor Penna*.

Figure 155.111. Classical figure emblematic of spring. H: 9". Companion subject to figures 55.108–111. "16" is painted on the back of the plinth. Grapes (autumn's attribute) are on the base, suggesting an error in manufacture. Price B. *Elinor Penna*.

Figure 155.112. Summer, spring, reverse of figures 155.110–111 showing "16" painted on the backs of each plinth. A pair of Flemish musicians occur on similar numbered plinths (Vol. 1, figs. 26.184–186). *Elinor Penna*.

Figure 155.113. *Winter, Autumn, Summer, Spring,* a set of classical figures. H: 10.2". From the same molds as figures 155.108–111, but the motifs on the pedestals are different. Price C, set. © *Lyon & Turnbull.*

Figure 155.114. Man wearing a long coat and warming his hands over a fire. Emblematic of winter. H: 12.8". Companion figures are not recorded. Price B. *The William Herbert and Nancy Hunt Collection.*

Figure 155.115. Man emblematic of winter. H: 7.6". Companion figureS are not recorded. Price A. *Bob Moores at Nestegg Antiques.*

Classical Subjects

156. Aesculapius

Earthenware figures of Aesculapius, the Greco-Roman god of medicine, portray him with the powerful frame and heavy head of hair familiar from ancient statuary, and holding a staff entwined with a single snake. This staff is the traditional symbol of medicine, and the use of a twin-snaked caduceus is a confused twentieth-century adaptation. The Derby porcelain figure of Aesculapius, made circa 1780, portrays a slender young man holding a scroll with a club at his side, and two earthenware figures of this form are recorded, both decorated in under-glaze colors.[1] Around 1793, Derby modified this model to include a serpent.[2]

Enamel-painted figures of Aesculapius are all from the same figure molds and are either made by John Dale or are attributable to the Brown Base Group. Interestingly, the same can be said of figures of Mercury (chap. 184). This invites conjecture that there is some linkage between Dale and the Brown Base Group. Brown Base Group figures seem to predate Dale figures by decade or two, so perhaps Dale acquired the Brown Base molds.

Figure 156.1. Aesculapius. Impressed "I. DALE BURSLEM". H: 9.3". Price B.

Figure 156.2. Aesculapius. Attributed to Brown Base Group. H: 8.5". Price B.

157. Agrippina with the Ashes of Germanicus

In 19 C.E., the Roman commander Germanicus died of poisoning, and Agrippina, his widow, brought his ashes home. This tragic subject was appealing in the neoclassical period. The figure of Agrippina derives from Alexander Runciman's print of circa 1773 titled *Agrippina with the Ashes of Germanicus*. Agrippina is found paired with the figure of Poor Maria (Vol. 2, chap. 41).

Figure 157.1. *Agrippina with the Ashes of Germanicus*, Alexander Runciman, circa 1773.

Figure 157.2. Agrippina with the ashes of Germanicus (L) and Poor Maria (R), a pair, each with a spill vase and bocage. H: ~8.5". Price B. *Andrew Dando Antiques.*

Figure 157.3. Agrippina with the ashes of Germanicus (L) and Poor Maria (R), a pair, each with a spill vase. H: 8". Price A. *Peter Flemans*.

Figure 157.4. Agrippina with the ashes of Germanicus, with a spill vase. H: 7.4". Incised "1804" beneath. Pairs with Poor Maria (Vol. 2, figs. 41.4–6). Price B. *Image courtesy of The Potteries Museum & Art Gallery, Stoke-on-Trent, UK*.

Figure 157.5. DetailS of the floral sprigs and the incised "1804" on the previous figure. The companion figure (Vol. 2, figs. 41.4–6) is incised "WL 1804". *Image courtesy of The Potteries Museum & Art Gallery, Stoke-on-Trent, UK*.

158. Andromache Weeping over the Ashes of Hector

The *Iliad* tells that Hector was killed in the Trojan War and his body was returned to his wife, Andromache. The figure of Andromache weeping over the ashes of Hector derives from the mezzotint of that title by Thomas Burke after Angelica Kauffman, 1771. By 1780, Derby and Bow had fashioned porcelain figures after the mezzotint, and these figures probably inspired earthenware look-alikes. Examples impressed "LEEDS POTTERY" are in the Victoria and Albert Museum (C.29-1955) and at Temple Newsam (16.197/47). Marked and unmarked figures of Andromache are indistinguishable from each other, and probably all were made at Leeds.

Figure 158.1. *Andromache Weeping Over the Ashes of Hector*, Thomas Burke after Angelica Kauffman, 1771.

Figure 158.2. Andromache weeping over the ashes of Hector. Probably made by the Leeds Pottery. H: 12.5". Price B. *Collection of Arnold and Barbara Berlin*.

159. Apollo

Apollo, the Greek god epitomizing male beauty, is portrayed in art as a slender youth. Earthenware figures of Apollo have him holding a lyre in his role of patron of music and leader of the Muses. Examples impressed "LAKIN & POOLE"[1] and "FELL"[2] (not shown here) seem to come from very similar molds to those used for the largest figures of Apollo shown below.

Figure 159.1. *Apollo*. Attributed to Ralph Wood; impressed "43". H: 8.8". A similar figure impressed "45" is recorded. Ralph Wood figures more commonly have red or red-brown lines and titles on their bases. Price A. *Bonhams*.

Figure 159.2. *Apollo*. Attributed to Ralph Wood. H: 8.7". Like the previous figure but not numbered. Titling is in red, as is more usual. The typical Ralph Wood "rainbow" palette is evident on the mound. Price A. © *Lyon & Turnbull*.

Figure 159.3. Apollo. H: 7.7". Price A. *Robert Hawker*.

Figure 159.4. Apollo. H: 7.4". Price A. *Aurea Carter Antiques*.

Figure 159.5. Apollo. H: 7.4". Price B. © *Victoria and Albert Museum, London*.

Figure 159.6. Apollo. Attributed to Brown Base Group. H: 13.4". Price B.

Figure 159.7. Apollo. Attributed to Brown Base Group. H: 13". The lyre is largely original and differs from that on the previous Apollo from the same pot bank. Price A.

Figure 159.8. Apollo. H: 12.7". Price B. *Aurea Carter Antiques*.

Figure 159.9. Apollo, base of previous figure. Despite the resemblance to the Brown Base Group figures, the base suggests some other pot bank made it. *Aurea Carter Antiques*.

Figure 159.10. Apollo. H: 14". Closely similar to the Brown Base Group figures., but the brighter palette suggests a slightly later date. Price B. *Phil Masters Antiques, Leek.*

Figure 159.11. Apollo. Possibly made by Lakin & Poole. H: 13.3". Price B. © *Fitzwilliam Museum, Cambridge.*

Figure 159.12. *APOLLO*. Impressed "NEALE & Co" and "APOLLO" beneath. H: 6". A similar figure with the Wilson mark is in the Fitzwilliam Museum (c.928–1928). Price B.

Figure 159.13. *APOLLO*. Attributed to Neale & Co/Wilson. H: 6". Impressed "APOLLO" beneath. Unmarked but of a quality that is at least as good as the marked Neale example in figure 159.12. Price A.

Figure 159.14. Apollo. H: 6". Figures of Ceres and figures emblematic of the seasons also occur on this base. Price A. *Elinor Penna*.

Figure 159.15. Candlestick flanked by Ceres and Apollo. H: 10.5". A candlestick from the same molds decorated in underglaze colors and inscribed "Wm Turner" is recorded.[3] Price B. *The William Herbert and Nancy Hunt Collection.*

Figure 159.16. Watch stand flanked by Ceres and Apollo. H: 9.5". Price B. *John Howard; www.antiquepottery.co.uk.*

160. Atlas

In mythology, Atlas helped the Titans rebel against Zeus. As punishment, he was sentenced to support the heavens with his head and hands. The Roman marble known as the *Farnese Atlas*, circa 150 C.E. and now in Naples, created the image of Atlas that has been reflected in art until today. A print or reduced-size plaster of this statue inspired the earthenware figure. All examples are traditionally attributed to Wood & Caldwell, without any basis for that attribution. Note that the figure holds a large globe formed from two molded parts. The purpose of the holes usually in the top of the globe is not known.

Figure 160.1. Atlas. Possibly made by Enoch Wood/Wood & Caldwell. H: 11". Price A. *Andrew Dando Antiques.*

Figure 160.2. Atlas. Possibly made by Enoch Wood/Wood & Caldwell. H: 11". Cursive "G" impressed beneath. Price A. *K. Stafford.*

Figure 160.3. Atlas. Possibly made by Enoch Wood/Wood & Caldwell. H: 11.3". This globe has a large opening at the top. Price A. *The William Herbert and Nancy Hunt Collection.*

Figure 160.4. Atlas. H: ~9.5". Possibly made by Enoch Wood/Wood & Caldwell. Differs from previous examples in that the globe is smaller (possibly with a large opening at the top) and is painted with lines suggestive of latitude and longitude. Price A.

161. Ariadne

Mythology tells that when Bacchus found the Cretian princess Ariadne abandoned and forlorn, he married her and made her immortal by placing her crown among the stars. The jewels in the crown were transformed into stars, thereby creating the constellation known as Corona. Figures of Ariadne are very rare. The only titled example is shown in figure 161.1.

The large lady in figures 161.5–6 is described in older literature as Purity, but there is no classical association for that naming. The figure is sometimes described as Hygeia, but again no basis for that naming is apparent. Because she stands like *Ariadne* in figure. 161.1 and she wears a crown of sorts, she is thought to portray Ariadne. This figure is usually attributed to Enoch Wood/Wood & Caldwell, but a marked example is not known.[1] A figure of the same form with an impressed "WEDGWOOD" mark is documented.[2]

Figure 161.1. *ARIADNE*. Attributed to Lakin & Poole. H: 12.3". This figure is also recorded untitled and with the Lakin & Poole mark.[3] Price B. © *Fitzwilliam Museum, Cambridge.*

Figure 161.2. Ariadne, front and reverse. Attributed to Enoch Wood. H: 5.4". Matches an unpainted excavated Enoch Wood figure (fig. 161.3). Styled after the Derby porcelain figure. Price A. *Image courtesy of The Potteries Museum & Art Gallery, Stoke-on-Trent, UK.*

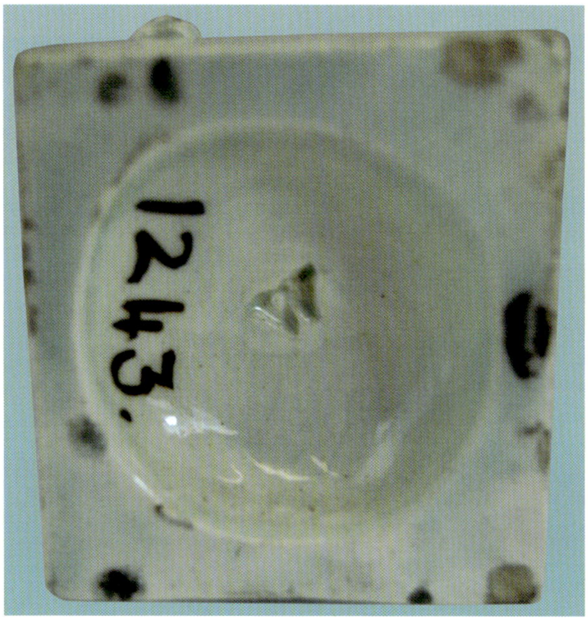

Figure 161.3. Ariadne. Attributed to Enoch Wood. H: 5.2". Excavated from the Enoch Wood Burslem Old Town Hall site. The base is impressed "W" beneath. Pairs with Bacchus (fig. 162.5). *Image courtesy of The Potteries Museum & Art Gallery, Stoke-on-Trent, UK.*

Figure 161.4. Ariadne. Attributed to Brown Base Group. H: 8.8". Price A.

Figure 161.5. Ariadne. Probably made by Enoch Wood/Wood & Caldwell. H: 27.7". This figure was made without the rectangular base present on the following similar figure. Price C. *Brighton and Hove Museums.*

Figure 161.6. Ariadne. Probably made by Enoch Wood/Wood & Caldwell. H: 28". Price C. *Skinner, Inc.; www.skinnerinc.com.*

162. Bacchus

Figures of Bacchus, the god of wine, are rare and are sometimes paired with Venus. In early artworks, Bacchus is depicted with both Venus and Ceres, the goddesses of love and food respectively. This presentation references a quotation from Terence, the 2nd century B.C.E. Latin poet, "Without Ceres and Bacchus, Venus would freeze". Put another way, without food and wine, love would grow cold.

A marble of Bacchus by the sixteenth-century Italian sculptor Sansovino inspired eighteenth-century porcelain figures. By the 1770s, Meissen, Bow, and Derby had transposed and adapted Sansovino's form to include drapery that concealed its nudity. These porcelain figures were paired with Ariadne, derived from an unknown source. Earthenware figures of Bacchus are also reminiscent of Sansovino's form but without the delicacy or excessive draping found in the earlier porcelain forms.

Figure 162.1. Venus and Bacchus, a pair. Both impressed "NEALE & Co". H: 8.7" (L), 8.9" (R). The mark is impressed on the front edge of both bases. Made without bocages. Price B. *Eileen and Robert Carde.*

Figure 162.2. Bacchus, reverse of previous figure. *Eileen and Robert Carde.*

Figure 162.3. *Venus, Baccus*; with bocages, a pair. Attributed to Ralph Wood. H: ~9". Bacchus occurs in colored glazes impressed "57"; Venus occurs impressed "52" or "57". Ralph Wood also made a figure of Venus beside a dolphin to stand with Neptune (chapter 194). Restored bocages. Price A.

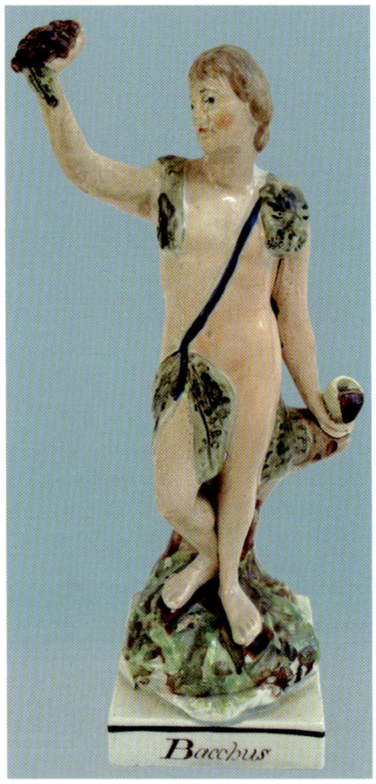

Figure 162.4. *Bacchus*. Attributed to Ralph Wood. H: ~8". Like the previous model but titled differently. The figure retains its elegance despite the loss of the bocage. Price A.

Figure 162.5. Bacchus. Attributed to Enoch Wood. H: 6". Excavated from the Burslem Old Town Hall site associated with Enoch Wood, circa 1820–30. Pairs with Ariadne (fig. 161.3). *Image courtesy of The Potteries Museum & Art Gallery, Stoke-on-Trent, UK.*

Figure 162.6. Bacchus. Probably made at the Leeds Pottery. H: 7.6". Made without bocage. The facial features suggest a Leeds source. Note the grapes on the base. A figure reproduced at Leeds from these molds circa 1900 is at Temple Newsam House (16.192/47). Price A. *Collection of Arnold and Barbara Berlin.*

Figure 162.7. Bacchus and Venus; with bocages. Attributed to Dale. H: ~7". The floral sprig on each base is characteristic of Dale, and the bocages are consistent with the attribution. Price B.

163. Bacchus and Ariadne

The figure group known as *Bacchus and Ariadne* is modeled after a Greco-Roman marble brought to Britain from Rome in about 1770, with both figures' heads and most limbs lost. The marble was restored incorrectly in the late eighteenth century to resemble Dionysus (also known as Bacchus) and Ariadne. The transformed marble gave rise to the pottery figure now known as Bacchus and Ariadne. Subsequently, the marble was identified as Priapus and a Maenad because a Greco-Roman marble in Athens has Priapus's head intact, and a group in Berlin preserves the maenad's head.

Apparently, more than one pot bank made Bacchus and Ariadne groups. All are large and most are painted in a delicate late eighteenth-century palette. Despite differences in the modeling, those on low rectangular bases are generally attributed to Enoch Wood/ Wood & Caldwell, but it is quite probable that more than one pot bank made them. Falkner notes an example in a private collection bearing the words "E. WOOD. Sculpt. E. HEWITT Pinxt".[1] Also, a silver luster example is in the Wood family vault, St. John's Church, Burslem. Possibly all Bacchus and Ariadne groups were derived from plaster casts, such as the plaster cast that Charles Harris of the Strand, London, advertised in his catalog of circa 1790.[2] It has been suggested that earthenware group of Bacchus and Ariadne paired with earthenware group of Cupid and Psyche because statuary examples were paired thus.[3]

Figure 163.1. Bacchus and Ariadne. H: 20.9". The particularly fine enamels in a circa 1790 palette are suggestive of Lakin & Poole or Neale. Price E. *Jonathan Horne.*

Figure 163.2. Bacchus and Ariadne. H: 22". Price E. *Jonathan Horne.*

Figure 163.3. Bacchus and Ariadne. H: 25.2". Probably made by Enoch Wood/Wood & Caldwell. From the same molds as used for the silver luster example in the Wood family vault, St. John's Church, Burslem. Price E. *Elinor Penna*.

Figure 163.4. Bacchus and Ariadne. Possibly made by Enoch Wood/Wood & Caldwell. H: 25". From slightly different molds than those used for figure 163.3 (the clothing drapes differently) and in a softer palette. Price E. *The William Herbert and Nancy Hunt Collection.*

Figure 163.5. Bacchus and Ariadne. H: 24". Figures of Prudence and Fortitude also occur on bases like this. Price D. *Collection of Arnold and Barbara Berlin*.

164. Calliope

Calliope is the muse of epic poetry. The figures shown are the only known examples. They are quite unlike early porcelain portrayals of Calliope, and a plaster or bronze derived from ancient statuary probably was their design source. The figures are decorated with silver luster and therefore were made after the introduction of silver lustering in 1805. Note that figures of Metis also stand with a large book (chapter 185).

Figure 164.1. Calliope, 2nd century Roman copy of a Greek statue, now in the Hermitage. © *Yair Haklai.*

Figure 164.2. Calliope. H: 13". The book is titled "OVID VOL 4" on the spine. Price B. © *Fitzwilliam Museum, Cambridge.*

Figure 164.3. Calliope. H: 12.8". The book is titled "OVID Vol 5" on the spine. Figure 195.12 shows Calliope's companion figure. Price B. *The William Herbert and Nancy Hunt Collection.*

165. Cephalus and Procris

In Greek mythology, Procris, jealous of her husband Cephalus, hides in a bush to watch him hunting. Cephalus, believing Procris's movements to be those of an animal, hurls his magic spear that never misses its mark at the bush and kills her. By the end of the sixteenth century, the tale was retold as an English poem, and it was also portrayed in classical art (notably *The Death of Procris* by Joachim Wtewael, circa 1595–1600). The story was revived as the pantomime *Cephalus and Procris* that first played at Drury Lane in 1733. Derby portrayed Cephalus and Procris in figural form from the late 1700s, but Staffordshire versions are markedly different.

No precise design source for earthenware groups of Cephalus and Procris has been identified, but the form seems to have been inspired by contemporary prints. All known examples of this figure were made by Lakin & Poole, a partnership that operated for fewer than five years.

Figure 165.1. *Cephalus & Procris*, Thomas Burke, 1790.

Figure 165.2. *CEPHALUS & PROCRIS*. Impressed "LAKIN & POOLE". H: 11". Price C.

166. Ceres or Plenty

Ceres was the Roman goddess of agriculture and abundance, and she is sometimes depicted with a wheat and sickle. Because she personifies the abundance of the earth, she has been portrayed for thousands of years with a cornucopia, a symbol of plenty. Neale & Co./Wilson figures of Ceres date from the early 1780s and frequently have *CERES* impressed beneath. Taller examples by other potters are sometimes titled *Plenty,* but are more frequently untitled. Figures of Ceres also occur as allegorical portrayals of summer in sets of figures emblematic of the four seasons (chapter 155).

Figure 166.1. *Ceres the Goddess of Plenty*, published by P. D. Dawe, 1810. Prints of this period often depict allegorical figures of Plenty and Ceres in interchangeable roles.

Figure 166.2. Ceres. H: 6". Enamel-painted shards matching the feet of this figure were excavated from the site of William Greatbatch's pot bank in Fenton (active 1762–1782). An animal face is beneath Ceres's left foot. Price A.

Figure 166.3. *CERES*. Impressed "NEALE & Co" and "CERES" beneath. H: 6". Price B.

Figure 166.4. *"CERES"*. Impressed beneath "C" (intended to be "G") with a crown and "CERES". H: 6.4". The mark is that of Robert Wilson. Price B. © *Fitzwilliam Museum, Cambridge.*

Figure 166.5. *CERES*. Impressed "CERES" beneath. Attributed to Neale & Co/Wilson. H: 6". Price A.

Figure 166.6. Ceres. H: 6". As in figure 166.1, there is a small animal beneath Ceres's left foot. Price A. *Elinor Penna.*

Figure 166.7. Ceres. H: 8". Here Ceres holds wheat and a sickle rather than a cornucopia. The black line bands the entire base. A similarly styled Pomona is shown in figure 171.16. Price A. Nicholas Frost Antiques.

Figure 166.8. *Seres*. Possibly made by Ralph Wood. H: 7". Stoneware body. Blue line on three sides of the base only. A similar untitled figure and a similarly styled Pomona, both possibly by Ralph Wood, are recorded. Price A. © *Victoria and Albert Museum, London.*

Figure 166.9. *Plenty.* Attributed to Ralph Wood. H: 10". Ralph Wood's figure titled *Fortune* uses the same molds (fig. 195.10). Price A. *Nick Burton.*

Figure 166.10. Ceres. H: 12.5". Note the rather underdeveloped cornucopia. Price A. *Image courtesy of The Potteries Museum & Art Gallery, Stoke-on-Trent, UK.*

Figure 166.11. Ceres, with a lamb. H: 13.5". Possibly intended to be Flora because of the flower in her hand. Pairs with a similarly styled figure of Pomona (fig. 171.15). Price A. *Image courtesy of The Potteries Museum & Art Gallery, Stoke-on-Trent, UK.*

Figure 166.12. Ceres. Attributed to Brown Base Group. H: 8.5". Price A.

Figure 166.13. Ceres. H: 8.5". Price A.

Figure 166.14. Ceres. H: 20.3". Price B. *Collection of Arnold and Barbara Berlin.*

Figure 166.15. Ceres. H: ~10". Price A. *Andrew Dando Antiques.*

Figure 166.16. Ceres. H: 10.5". Price A. *M. J. Meehan.*

Figure 166.17. Ceres. Impressed "WOOD & CALDWELL". H: 10.7". From the same molds as the previous two figures, but here the cornucopia has been adapted to serve as a candle holder. A companion figure with the candle holder to the other side has been noted. Price A. *Aurea Carter Antiques.*

Figure 166.18. Ceres, base of the previous figure, impressed "WOOD & CALDWELL".

Figure 166.19. Ceres. Impressed "WOOD & CALDWELL". H: ~10". Differs from the preceding figures in that the cornucopia is held to the other side. Price A.

Figure 166.20. Ceres. H: 10". The cornucopia is modeled differently from the cornucopia in the previous figure. Price A. *Brighton and Hove Museums.*

Figure 166.21. Ceres, her horn of plenty formed as a vase. Impressed "TURNER" beneath; a small gold anchor painted beneath. H: 7". Price B.

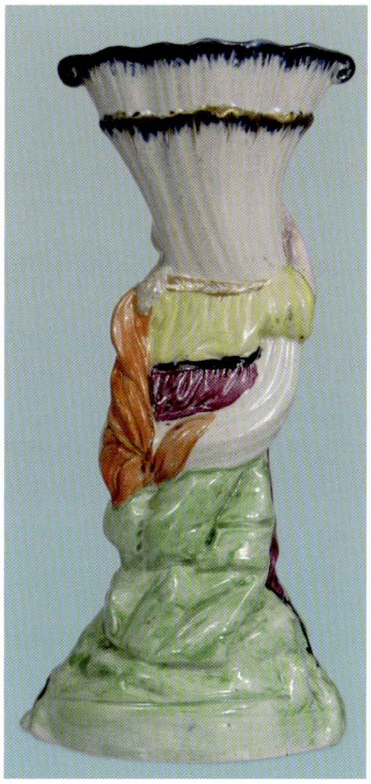

Figure 166.22. Ceres, reverse of the previous vase.

Figure 166.23. Ceres, her horn of plenty formed as a vase; with bocage. H: 8". Price A. *Barbara Gair; www.castle-antiques.com.*

Figure 166.24. Ceres, her horn of plenty formed as a vase, two examples. H: 7.5". Price A, each. *Martyn Edgell Antiques Ltd.*

Figure 166.25. Ceres, her horn of plenty formed as a vase. Attributed to "Sherratt". H: 7.5". The floral sprigs applied to the base are characteristic of "Sherratt". Price A.

Figure 166.26. Ceres. Attributed to "Sherratt". H: ~7.5". This figure model is an adaptation of the "Sherratt" figure of Flora (figs. 171.22–24). Price A.

Figure 166.27. Ceres. Attributed to "Sherratt". H: ~7.5". Like the previous figure but on a different "Sherratt" base. This figure, like the "Sherratt" Flora, stands well with the "Sherratt" Pomona (fig. 171.25). Price A.

Figure 166.28. Ceres. H: 5.8". Price A.

Figure 166.29. Ceres. H: 5.6". Price A. *Jack Hardin.*

167. Cupid and Psyche

Lucius Apuleius's second-century fable "Golden Ass" tells the story of the lovers Cupid and Psyche. The tall figure group of Cupid and Psyche in figure 167.2 was probably made circa 1790 after the statue of Cupid and Psyche in the Capitoline Museum Rome, with the assistance of a plaster. The London cast maker Charles Harris of the Strand included a twenty-one inch plaster of Cupid and Psyche in his catalogue of this period.[1] The design source of the smaller figure group (figs. 167.3–4) is not known.

Figure 167.1. Statue of *Cupid and Psyche* in the Capitoline Museum, Rome. © *Rosemania.*

Figure 167.2. Cupid and Psyche. H: 20.4". Price C. © *Fitzwilliam Museum, Cambridge.*

Figure 167.3. Cupid and Psyche. Attributed to Lakin & Poole. H: 9.9". Made without a square base. This group is recorded impressed "LAKIN & POOLE". Price B.

Figure 167.4. Cupid and Psyche. Attributed to Lakin & Poole. H: 10.8". Price B. *The William Herbert and Nancy Hunt Collection.*

168. Demosthenes

Demosthenes (384–322 B.C.E.) was ancient Greece's greatest orator. He practiced with pebbles in his mouth to lessen his stuttering, and he addressed the roaring ocean to improve his volume. The plinth alongside figures of Demosthenes shows Mercury (the messenger of the Gods, associated with eloquence and reason) hovering over Demosthenes, who is speaking to the waves. The figure is sometimes described as *Eloquence*, sometimes as *St. Paul Preaching at Athens*, but nothing supports these titles. The figure occurs marked E. WOOD.[1] Possible design sources include a plaster, perhaps by John Cheere (d. 1787) or Charles Harris (d. circa 1795). It has been suggested that Peter Paul Rubens' painting of *The Vision of St. Augustine* influenced the design.[2]

Figure 168.1. Demosthenes. Possibly made by Enoch Wood/Wood & Caldwell. H: 18.7". Price D. *Andrew Dando Antiques.*

Figure 168.2. Detail of the frieze on the plinth of the previous example showing Mercury hovering over Demosthenes, who is addressing the waves. *Andrew Dando Antiques.*

Figure 168.3. Demosthenes. Possibly made by Enoch Wood/Wood & Caldwell. H: 18.4". Price D. *Elinor Penna.*

Figure 168.4. Demosthenes. Possibly made by Enoch Wood/ Wood & Caldwell. H: 18.5". Price D. © *Victoria and Albert Museum, London.*

169. Diana

In mythology, Diana, the goddess of the hunt and the moon, personifies chastity. Earthenware figures usually portray her wearing a crescent moon in her hair and carrying a bow and quiver. Their design source is not known, but most are in the style of earlier Derby porcelain figures of Diana.

Figure 169.1. *Diana*. Attributed to Ralph Wood; impressed "44". H: 8.8". Price A. *Bonhams*.

Figure 169.2. Diana. Attributed to Ralph Wood. H: ~10". The palette of the mound and the line banding three sides of the base are typical Ralph Wood features. Price A.

Figure 169.3. Diana. Impressed "W". Possibly made by Enoch Wood. H: 10.7". An impressed "W" is recorded on an Enoch Wood shard in the Potteries Museum (fig. 161.3). Some Ralph Wood figures are marked "W", but this figure lacks Ralph Wood features. Price A. *Aurea Carter Antiques*.

Figure 169.5. Diana. Possibly made by Enoch Wood. H: 11.5". The base is narrower than on previous examples. The leaves and flowers on the mound are suggestive of Enoch Wood. Price A. *Image courtesy of The Potteries Museum & Art Gallery, Stoke-on-Trent, UK.*

Figure 169.4. Diana. H: 11.4". Price A.

Figure 169.6. Diana. H: 11.2". Price A. *Collection of Michael J. Smith.*

Figure 169.7. Diana with dog; with bocage. Probably made by Enoch Wood. H: 11.3". On this model, the larger mound accommodates a recumbent dog. This base and these bocage fronds (each comprising seven fern leaflets, restored fronds on the left) are on other Enoch Wood figures. Price A.

Figure 169.8. Diana with dog; with bocage. Probably made by Enoch Wood. H: 11.3". Like the previous figure but with a different bocage (oak leaves with yellow and brown acorns) associated with Enoch Wood. Price A.

Figure 169.9. Diana. Impressed "WALTON". H: 11.6". Made without bocage. One of the few Walton figures without bocage and perhaps dating from earlier in the Walton period. This is the only marked Walton figure recorded on a brown base. Price A.

Figure 169.10. Diana. Impressed "WALTON". Made without bocage. H: 11.6". Like the previous figure but painted in a more typical Walton palette. Square bases are uncommon on Walton figures. Price A.

Figure 169.11. Diana; with bocage. Impressed "WALTON". H: ~12". Like the previous figure but with a bocage. Price B. *Holloway's, Banbury, England.*

Figure 169.12. Diana, with dog. Impressed "WALTON". H: 11.6". Price A. Made without bocage. *Elinor Penna.*

Figure 169.13. Diana with dog. Attributed to Brown Base Group. H: 9.2". Price B.

Figure 169.14. Diana. H: 11". The figure was made without a bocage, but leaves were placed along the stump behind it. Price A. *Image courtesy of The Potteries Museum & Art Gallery, Stoke-on-Trent, UK.*

Figure 169.15. Diana with dog. H: 10.3". Price A. *Andrew Dando Antiques.*

Figure 169.16. Diana with dog. Probably made by the Leeds Pottery. H: 7.6". There is gilding on the band with a crescent moon atop her head. The base is open beneath. Price B. *Image courtesy of The Potteries Museum & Art Gallery, Stoke-on-Trent, UK.*

Figure 169.17. Diana with dog. H: ~11". From the same molds as the Ralph Wood figure in figure 169.1, but the pink luster decoration indicates later (post 1805) manufacture. Price A.

170. Europa

In mythology, Zeus spied Europa gathering flowers and, smitten by her beauty, came to her disguised as a docile bull. When she clambered on his back to adorn his horns with garlands, he plunged into the ocean and bore her home to Crete. Europa thereby gave her name to the continent that included the Greek mainland. Artworks depicting this myth predate the Christian era, and by 1751, the "Girl-in-a-swing" factory had portrayed the myth in porcelain. The design source for the earthenware figures is not known, and the figures are known from only these examples.

Figure 170.1. Europa with the bull. H: 10.2". Figures of Elijah, Jupiter, and Liberty (Vol. 2, fig. 90.52, and figs. 177.9, 180.1) have closely similar patterns on the clothing. Price B.

Figure 170.2. Europa with the bull. Attributed to Brown Base Group. H: 8.6", L: 7.1". Europa has typical Brown Base facial features. Price B. *Clars Auction Galleries.*

Figure 170.3. Europa with the bull, base of the previous example showing the scored internal corners typical of Brown Base bases. *Clars Auction Galleries.*

171. Flora and Pomona

Flora was the Roman goddess of flowering trees and flowers. Earthenware figures of Flora are probably after earlier English porcelain figures derived from two sources: Italy's famous ancient Roman marble of Flora, which was much copied in two- and three-dimensional art works of the eighteenth century; and a print, *An Opera Girl of Paris in the Character of Flora*, published in 1771.

Pomona was the Roman goddess who cared for fruit trees, and, as their success depended on blooming, Pomona's task was the end process of Flora's work. Contemporary prints probably assisted in modeling figures of Pomona.

Figure 171.1. *An Opera Girl of Paris in the Character of Flora*, by Grignion after Brandoin, published by Robert Sayer, 1771.

Figure 171.2. *Pomona Goddess of Fruits*, P. Stampa, 1800.

Figure 171.3. Flora. H: 4.9". Pairs with the following figure of Pomona. Price A.

Figure 171.4. Pomona. H: 5.2". Pairs with the previous figure of Flora. Price A.

Figure 171.5. Flora. Attributed to Dudson. H: 6.8". There are typical Dudson x-sprigs within the garland. Pairs with the following Pomona. Price A. *Aurea Carter Antiques*.

Figure 171.6. Pomona. Attributed to Dudson. H: 6.8". Pairs with the previous Flora, the position of the garland being reversed. The apples in the garland signify that this figure is Pomona. Partial x-sprigs are within the garland. Price A. *Aurea Carter Antiques*.

Figure 171.7. Pomona, reverse of previous figure. *Aurea Carter Antiques*.

Figure 171.8. Pomona. Probably made by Dudson. H: ~6.8". Like the previous Pomona, and the garland has apples in it. Price A.

Figure 171.9. Flora. Attributed to Enoch Wood/Wood & Caldwell. H: 12". The large four-petalled flowers and the base support the attribution. Price A. *Aurea Carter Antiques*.

Figure 171.10. Flora. Attributed to Enoch Wood/Wood & Caldwell. H: 12.4". Like the previous figure but on a different base. The large flowers within the garland are characteristic of this pot bank. Price A. *Aurea Carter Antiques*.

Figure 171.11. Flora, with a sheep. H: 11.3". The body is porcelainous. Price B. *Geoffrey Godden Reference Collection, the Potteries Museum.*

Figure 171.12. Flora. H: ~10.5". Price A.

Figure 171.13. Flora. H: 7.5". Base lost. Price A. *Image courtesy of The Potteries Museum & Art Gallery, Stoke-on-Trent, UK.*

Figure 171.14. Flora, with a sheep. H: ~13.2". A similar figure is titled *Floro* on the mound (Fitzwilliam Museum C.1118–1928). Another titled *Florow* in the National Museum of Wales is attributed by the museum to the Cambrian Pottery. A similar porcelain figure is attributed to William Cookworthy at Bristol (1770–1780). Price B.

Figure 171.15. Flora, with dog. H: 12.6". Objects lost from both hands. A companion figure holding a flower and a large cornucopia probably represents Ceres (fig. 166.11). Price A. *Image courtesy of The Potteries Museum & Art Gallery, Stoke-on-Trent, UK.*

Figure 171.16. Pomona. Possibly made by Ralph Wood. Lines are painted on three sides of the base. There are similarly styled figures of Ceres (figs 166.7–8). Price A.

Figure 171.17. Flora. Attributed to "Sherratt". H: 7". Pairs with the following Pomona. Characteristic "Sherratt" sprigs are in the garland. Price B, pair.

Figure 171.18. Pomona. Attributed to "Sherratt". H: 7.2". Pairs with the previous Flora. Characteristic "Sherratt" sprigs are on the base. Price B, pair.

Figure 171.19. Flora and Pomona, reverse of previous two figures.

Figure 171.20. Pomona. Attributed to "Sherratt". H: 7.2". Like the previous figure of Pomona but painted quite differently and also made without a bocage. Price A. *John Howard; www.antiquepottery.co.uk.*

Figure 171.21. Pomona; with bocage. Attributed to "Sherratt". H: 7.8". Pairs with the following Flora. Price A.

Figure 171.22. Flora; with bocage. Attributed to "Sherratt". H: ~7.6". Pairs with the previous Pomona. Price A.

Figure 171.23. Flora; with bocage. Attributed to "Sherratt". H: ~7.6". A companion subject to Pomona in figure 171.21, but the base is painted in a different typical "Sherratt" manner. Price A.

Figure 171.24. Flora; with bocage. Attributed to "Sherratt". H: ~7.6". Like previous "Sherratt" figures of Flora but with fern-leaf bocage fronds. Price A.

Figure 171.25. Ceres (L) and Pomona (R). Attributed to "Sherratt". H: ~7.5". Made without bocages. Ceres is from the same molds as Flora, with slight adaptations. Price B.

Figure 171.26. Flora; with bocage. Attributed to "Sherratt". H: ~6". Smaller than previous "Sherratt" figures of Flora. There is no loss to the base. Price A.

Figure 171.27. Pomona; with bocage. Attributed to "Sherratt". H: 6.7". The bocage is typical of "Sherratt," as is the use of luster decoration. Price A.

Figure 171.28. Pomona. Impressed "NEALE & Co". H: 4.8". A rare figure. Neale also made a figure of Actaeon on the same scale.[1] Price B.

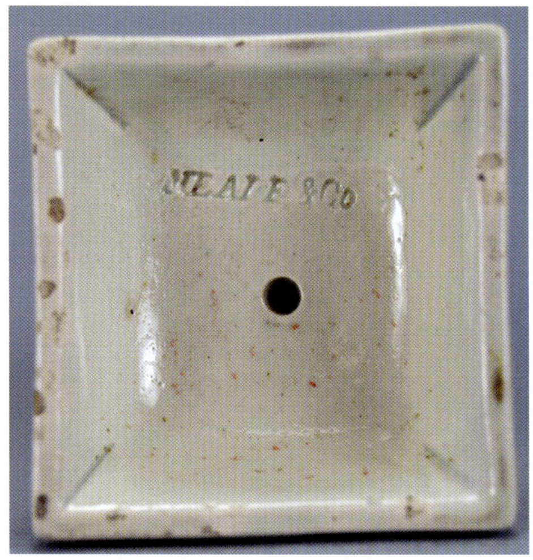

Figure 171.29. Base of previous figure showing the "NEALE & Co" mark and scored internal corners.

Figure 171.30. Pomona (R) and Actaeon (L). H: ~5". Actaeon is a hunter who is transformed into a stag. Both figures appear to be crude versions of Neale figures of these subjects. Price A.

172. Fortitude and Prudence

Fortitude and Prudence are two of the four cardinal virtues identified by Plato and adopted by Christianity. Earthenware depictions portray Prudence holding a mirror (implying the wisdom of self-knowledge) and a snake (from Matthew 10:16: "be ye wise as serpents," with the Latin word for "wise" being "prudentes"). Fortitude holds a broken pillar to represent her strength.[1]

The most well-known earthenware figures of Fortitude and Prudence are large statuesque forms that were probably made as a pair. They are traditionally attributed to Enoch Wood/Wood & Caldwell, but they apparently emanated from more than one pot bank. A pair impressed "E. WOOD" has been recorded,[2] as has a bronze-glazed example impressed "WOOD & CALDWELL".[3] A pair described as marked Wedgwood is in the Earle Collection (no. 422 and no. 426). The design sources for these figures are probably plasters from one of the London plaster makers. The most well-known marbles of Fortitude and Prudence are in St. Peter's Basilica, Rome. England, however, has its own representations: a monument to Lady Digges at the Parish Church of St. Mary's, Chilham, erected in 1631, portrays the cardinal virtues in figural form.

Figure 172.1. Prudence. Impressed "NEALE & Co". H: 7.7". A rare figure and much smaller than the following figures of Prudence. Price B.

Figure 172.2. Fortitude. Possibly made by Enoch Wood/Wood & Caldwell. H: 21". Price D. *Elinor Penna*.

Figure 172.3. Fortitude. Possibly made by Enoch Wood/Wood & Caldwell. H: 23.5". Price D. © *Victoria and Albert Museum, London*.

Figure 172.4. Prudence. Possibly made by Enoch Wood /Wood & Caldwell. H: 22.4". Price D. *Elinor Penna*.

Figure 172.6. Fortitude. Possibly made by Enoch Wood/Wood & Caldwell. H: 22". Price D. *Skinner, Inc.; www.skinnerinc.com.*

Figure 172.5. Prudence. H: 23". Fortitude also occurs on this base, as does Bacchus with Ariadne. Price D. *Collection of Arnold and Barbara Berlin.*

Figure 172.8. Fortitude. H: 6.2". An unusual small model known from only this example. Price A. *Aurea Carter.*

Figure 172.7. Prudence. H: ~20". With losses. Price B.

173. Ganymede

Ganymede was a Trojan prince of such beauty that Jupiter fell in love with him. Ovid tells that Jupiter changed himself into an eagle and bore Ganymede to Olympus. Here Ganymede became cup-bearer to the gods. The figure of Ganymede has an eagle (for Jupiter) and a cup (denoting Ganymede's role as cup-bearer). As in Roman era art, Ganymede wears a Phrygian cap, reflecting his Phrygian roots. Figures of Ganymede are rare, and only four enamel-painted examples have hitherto been recorded.

Figure 173.1. *GANYMEDE*. Attributed to Lakin & Poole. H: 13.4". Price B.

Figure 173.2. Ganymede. Impressed "LAKIN & POOLE". H: 13.2". The eagle is lost. Price B. *M. J. Meehan.*

174. Hercules

In ancient times, the god Hercules personified courage. Hercules wrestled Achelous for the love of Deianira and, although Achelous assumed the form of a bull, Hercules prevailed. In classical art, their struggle shows Hercules pressing his knee into the bull's back and holding its horns, and figure 174.2 portrays Hercules thus.

The large standing figures of Hercules (figs. 174.4–10) derive from the much-copied *Farnese Hercules* (now in the Naples National Archaeological Museum) but with the addition of foliage to conceal nudity. Here Hercules clutches behind his back the apples of Hesperides, which he gained executing one of the twelve labors he undertook as penance for slaying his children. A bronze or plaster was probably this figure model's design source.

Figure 174.1. *Hercule et Achelous*, after Giovanni Antonio Pordenone, 1790–1810.

Figure 174.2. Hercules wrestling Achelous. Attributed to Enoch Wood/ Wood & Caldwell. H: 5.3". A London retailer named Wyllie recorded in his ledger of November 25, 1815, that Wood & Caldwell supplied "1 Hercules and Bull" for 2 shillings and sixpence. Price B. *Andrew Dando Antiques.*

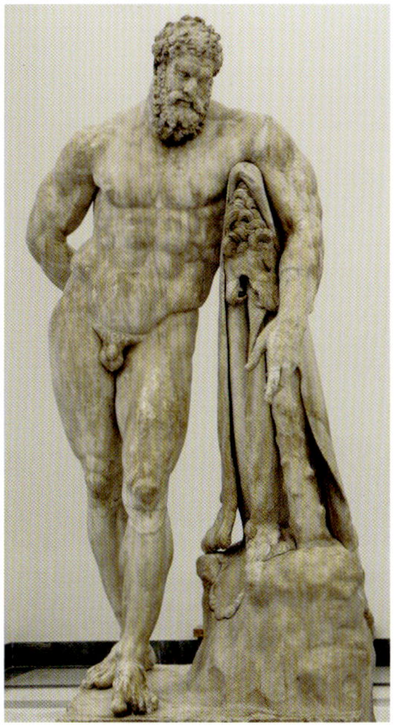

Figure 174.3. *Farnese Hercules*, now in the Naples National Archaeological Museum. ©*Marie-Lan Nguyen.*

Figure 174.4. Hercules. Impressed "Ra. Wood Burslem" and "103". H: 18.5". Price D. *Jonathan Horne.*

Figure 174.5. Hercules. H: 17.3". Price D. *Image courtesy of The Potteries Museum & Art Gallery, Stoke-on-Trent, UK.*

Figure 174.6. Hercules, reverse of the previous figure. As in all figures shown here, Hercules holds the apples of Hesperides behind his back.

Figure 174.7. Hercules. H: 17.3". Slightly later in date than the Ralph Wood figure in 174.4 but seemingly from the same molds or plaster source. Price C. *Image courtesy of The Potteries Museum & Art Gallery, Stoke-on-Trent, UK.*

Figure 174.8. Hercules. H: 16.8". All figures of this form are closely similar and may derive from the same molds or plaster source. Price D. *Image courtesy of The Potteries Museum & Art Gallery, Stoke-on-Trent, UK.*

Figure 174.10. Hercules. H: 17.8". Like the previous example, but Hercules holds a small animal (like that on the base of the previous figure) in his left hand. Price D. *Image courtesy of The Potteries Museum & Art Gallery, Stoke-on-Trent, UK.*

Figure 174.9. Detail of the base of the previous figure. Small dolphins and an animal (perhaps a bird) decorate the base. *Image courtesy of The Potteries Museum & Art Gallery, Stoke-on-Trent, UK.*

175. Hygeia

Hygeia was the goddess of health. She healed the sick by administering the bile of the gorgon Medusa, and, for that reason, she is depicted with a ewer and bowl holding Medusa's bile. In ancient statuary, Hygeia frequently feeds a snake from a bowl, the snake symbolizing healing or rebirth because of its ability to shed its skin. By 1780, the Derby porcelain factory had made Hygeia to pair with Aesculapius, and the porcelain form probably inspired earthenware figures.

Figure 175.1. Hygeia. H: 9.5". Price A. *Andrew Dando Antiques.*

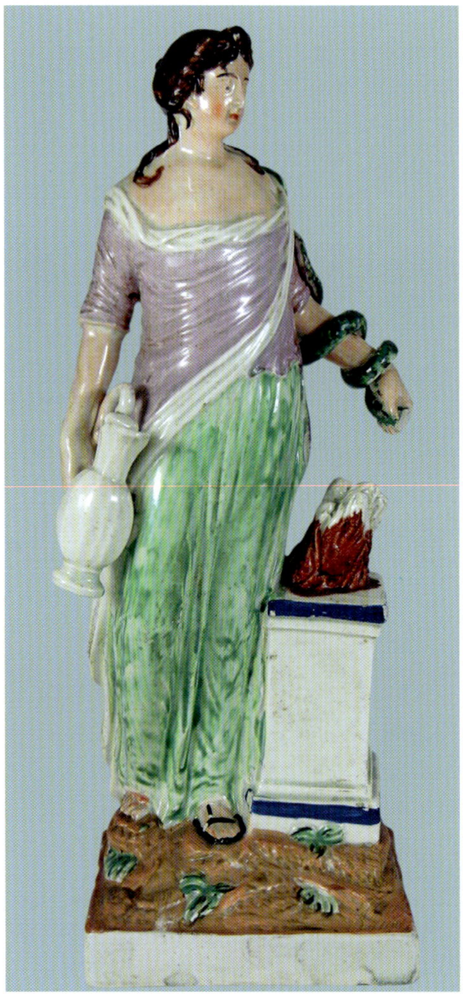

Figure 175.2. Hygeia. H: 9.2". Price A. *Brighton and Hove Museums.*

Figure 175.3. Hygeia; with bocage. Possibly made by Enoch Wood. H: ~10". Bocage restored after a form specific to Enoch Wood. Price A.

176. Jason and Medea

The Greek hero Jason led the Argonauts on their voyage to capture the Golden Fleece from the king of Colchis. Medea, the king's daughter, was a witch, and she helped Jason in his quest and returned to Greece with him to become his wife. Circa 1770–1790, the Derby factory made a pair of porcelain figures (sometimes dubbed "sacrifice" figures) depicting Jason and Medea. The Derby male appears to have been the prototype for the Staffordshire male, but there is little resemblance between the female porcelain and earthenware figures. Bradshaw traces the male figures to Charles Monnet's engraving *Jason and Medea at the Altar of Diana* that illustrates *Les Metamorphoses d'Ovide* by L'Abbe Bannier, Paris, 1767–1771.[1] Although this engraving inspired a composite Derby sacrifice group, its association with individual figures of either Jason or Medea is tenuous.

Figure 176.1. Jason. H: 8". Price A. *Newcastle-under-Lyme Museum.*

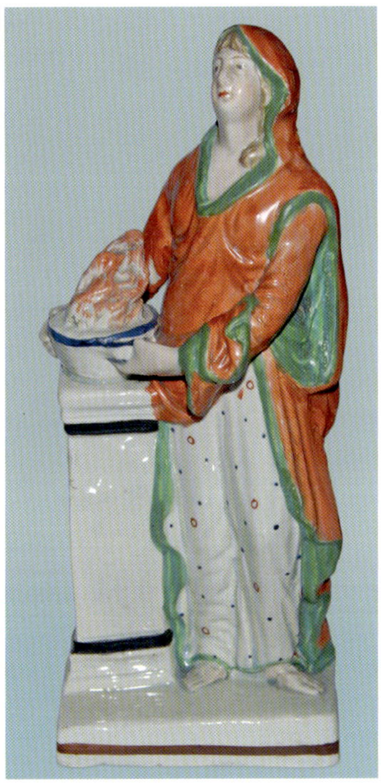

Figure 176.2. Medea. Possibly made by Enoch Wood. H: 8". A partial figure of this form was excavated from the St. Paul's Churchyard site associated with Enoch Wood, but several pot banks seem to have produced closely similar figures. Price A. *Elinor Penna.*

Figure 176.3. Medea. H: 8". The open base is not typical of Enoch Wood, and some other pot bank probably made this figure. Price A.

Figure 176.4. Jason and Medea. H: 8" (L) and 8.1" (R). Price B. *Collection of Arnold and Barbara Berlin.*

Figure 176.5. Jason. H: 8". Facial features and the base hint at a Lakin & Poole attribution. The enamel palette suggests late eighteenth-century manufacture. Price A.

Figure 176.6. Jason. H: 8.5". Jason's head and the bowl (now fluted) differ from the head and bowl on previous examples. Price A. *Collection of Arnold and Barbara Berlin.*

177. Jupiter and Juno

Jupiter and Juno were the chief Roman god and goddess. They were also both husband and wife and brother and sister. Jupiter's attributes include an eagle and thunderbolts (the sticks he holds), and Juno's attribute is usually a peacock. The earthenware figures are after early Derby porcelain figures.

Figure 177.1. Jupiter. H: 6.5". Very like the contemporary Derby porcelain figure. Companion to the following Juno. Price A. *Collection of Michael J. Smith.*

Figure 177.2. Juno. H: ~5.7". Companion to the previous Jupiter. Very like the contemporary Derby porcelain figure. Price A.

Figure 177.3. *Jupiter.* Attributed to Ralph Wood. H: 10.5". Occurs in colored glazes impressed "79". An enamel-painted example of this figure with an impressed number is not recorded. Price B. *Robert Hawker.*

Figure 177.4. *Jupiter.* Attributed to Ralph Wood; impressed "78". H: 11.4". This model differs from the Ralph Wood model of Jupiter in figure 177.3. Price B. *Bonhams.*

Figure 177.5. *Jupiter.* Attributed to Ralph Wood. H: 11.2". *Jupiter* is painted beneath. Incorrectly titled *Hercules* on the front, and the base was then painted with black to conceal the mistake. Two examples are recorded with this error and correction. Price B.

Figure 177.6. *Jupiter.* H: 13.2". Titled *Jupiter* inside the wall of the base. Several other large figures on similar plinths (Dr. Franklin, St. John, and St. Peter) are also titled in slightly different hands within. Price B. *Aurea Carter Antiques.*

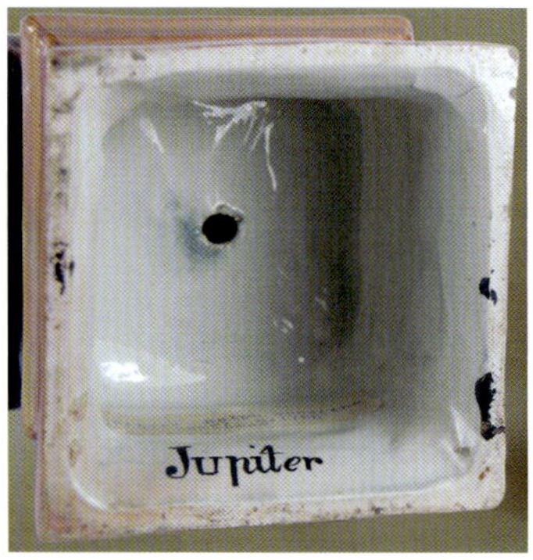

Figure 177.7. *Jupiter,* previous example showing titling within the base. The script is very like that found on Dudson figures.

Figure 177.8. *Jupiter.* Probably made by Dudson. H: 9.3". The titling is typical of that on Dudson figures. Price A.

Figure 177.9. Jupiter. H: 16.5". Very unusual in that transfer-printed designs are on all sides of the pediment. Price C. *Collection of Arnold and Barbara Berlin.*

Figure 177.10. Jupiter, reverse of previous example. *Collection of Arnold and Barbara Berlin.*

Figure 177.11. Details of the transfer print designs around the pediment of the previous figure of Jupiter. See figure 129.7 in Volume 3 for similar decoration. *Collection of Arnold and Barbara Berlin.*

Figure 177.12. Jupiter. H: 8.5". Price A. *Image courtesy of The Potteries Museum & Art Gallery, Stoke-on-Trent, UK.*

Figure 177.13. Jupiter. H: 11". Price A. *Andrew Dando Antiques.*

Figure 177.14. Jupiter. Attributed to Brown Base Group. H: 14.5". Price B.

Figure 177.15. Jupiter. Attributed to Brown Base Group. H: 9.2". Significantly smaller than the previous example and a companion to the following figure of Juno. Price A.

Figure 177.16. Juno. Attributed to Brown Base Group. H: 8.8". A companion to the previous example of Jupiter. Price B.

Figure 177.17. Juno. Attributed to Dale. H: ~9.3". Same figure form as the previous Juno, but the peacocks' tails differ. The floral sprigs on the base are specific to Dale. Price B.

Figure 177.18. *Juno* (painted on the back). H: 8.7". Uses the same body molds as the previous two figures, but the head differs. Appears to be a late eighteenth century figure, possibly made by Brown Base Group or Lakin & Poole. Price A. *Image courtesy of The Potteries Museum & Art Gallery, Stoke-on-Trent, UK.*

Figure 177.19. *Juno*, reverse of previous figure. "83" is incised on the reverse of the peacock's tail. The back of the base is not marbled, suggesting a Lakin & Poole linkage. *Image courtesy of The Potteries Museum & Art Gallery, Stoke-on-Trent, UK.*

Figure 177.20. *Juno*, base of previous figure. The internal corners of the base are consistent with a Lakin & Poole or Brown Base attribution. *Image courtesy of The Potteries Museum & Art Gallery, Stoke-on-Trent, UK.*

178. Justice

From Roman times, Justice has been depicted holding scales to denote her impartiality, and her blindfold, added later, has the same symbolism. She also traditionally holds a sword to signify her power. By 1770, Derby had fashioned figures of Justice that were the design source for the earthenware figures subsequently created by Staffordshire's potters. These figures are surprisingly uncommon and appear to be companions to figures of Peace (chapter 188).

Figure 178.1. Justice. Possibly made by Enoch Wood. H: 9". There should be scales in her left hand. Price A. © *Victoria and Albert Museum, London*.

Figure 178.2. Justice. H: 8.6". A rare figure. Companion to Peace (fig. 188.2). Price B.

179. Leda and the Swan

Greek mythology tells that Jupiter came to Leda, wife of the King of Sparta, in the form of a swan. As a result of their union, Leda laid an egg from which the heavenly twins Castor and Pollux hatched. This myth was prominent in Renaissance art.

Figure 179.1. Leda and the Swan. Attributed to Brown Base Group. H: 7.5". Price B.

180. Liberty

After the abolition of the French monarchy, the Convention of 1792 decreed that a figure of Liberty should appear on the French Republic's new Seal of State. Liberty is portrayed on the seal as a lady wearing a crown and holding fasces in her right hand to symbolize the power of the liberated people. In ancient Rome, fasces conveyed the power of Roman magistrates to punish. They comprised a bundle of birch rods tied into a cylinder with a leather ribbon, and an axe sometimes protruded from amongst the rods. A depiction of Liberty—in print or figural form, as on the French Seal of State—probably inspired the earthenware figure.

Figure 180.1. Liberty. H: 10.5". The elaborate dress pattern is closely similar to that on the clothing of figures of Europa, Elijah, and Jupiter (Vol. 2, fig. 90.52, and figs. 170.1, 177.9). Price B. © *Victoria and Albert Museum, London*.

181. Lucretia

According to Ovid's *Fasti* and Livy's *History of Rome*, in 509 B.C.E., the son of the king of Rome raped Lucretia, and she committed suicide out of shame. Lucretia's death incited the overthrow of the royal family, resulting in the establishment of the Roman republic. "The Rape of Lucrece," a poem by Shakespeare, and Baroque art revived the tale. In earthenware figures, Lucretia's face is concealed to indicate her shame. The figure's design source is not known.

Figure 181.1. Lucretia. L: 10.2". Price B. *Collection of Arnold and Barbara Berlin*.

Figure 181.2. Lucretia. L: 13.7". Price B. © *Victoria and Albert Museum, London*.

Figure 181.3. *LUCRETIA*. Impressed "WEDGWOOD". L: 10". Price B. *Skinner, Inc.; www.skinnerinc.com.*

182. Mars

Mars was the Roman god of war. His aggressive nature made him hated by all except Venus, and she fell in love with him. Porcelain figures of Mars date from the Meissen model of the 1740s, and these were quickly followed by similar models from Derby, Bow, and Chelsea. A figure of Mars at Temple Newsam House (16.200/47) is impressed "LEEDS POTTERY".

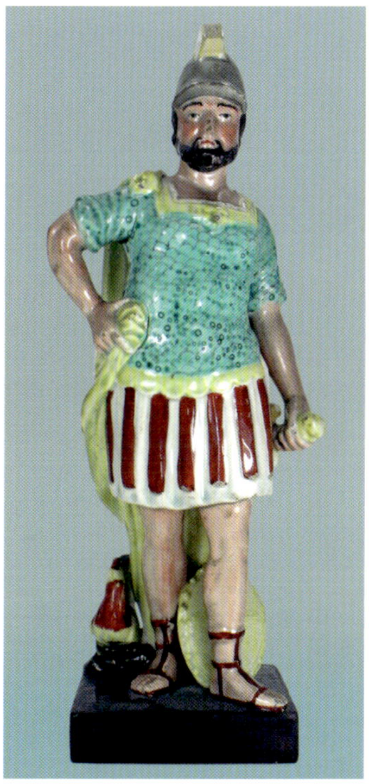

Figure 182.1. Mars. Attributed to Brown Base Group. H: 9.4". Price B.

Figure 182.2. *MARS* (painted on the back). Possibly attributable to Brown Base Group or Lakin & Poole. H: 9.4". Like the previous figure, but the back of the base is not marbled, suggesting a Lakin & Poole linkage. Appears to pair with Minerva in figure 186.5. Price B. *John Howard; www.antiquepottery.co.uk.*

Figure 182.3. *MARS*, reverse of the previous figure. A figure of Juno (fig. 177.18) is also titled on the back. *John Howard; www.antiquepottery.co.uk.*

Figure 182.5. Mars. Possibly made by Enoch Wood/Wood & Caldwell. H: 26". Price C.

Figure 182.4. Base of previous figure of Mars. The tooled internal corners are consistent with either a Brown Base Group or Lakin and Poole attribution. *John Howard; www.antiquepottery.co.uk.*

183. Melpomene and Thalia

Mythology tells that Zeus and Mnemosyne slept together for nine consecutive nights, thus creating the nine muses. The muses of comedy and tragedy, also known as Thalia and Melpomene, have been represented in art since ancient times. Their attributes traditionally included masks, but in later centuries they came to include pertinent stage props. Most earthenware figures portray both muses in a homely style, with Melpomene beside a tombstone ("Memento" may be painted on it), and the titles *TRAGEDY* and *COMEDY* are sometimes impressed into the bases.

Figure 183.1. Melpomene, 50 B.C.E., now in the Louvre. © *Sting (Eric Gaba).*

Figure 183.2. Melpomene. H: 6". After the ancient classical statue. A rare figure. Price A.

Figure 183.3. *TRAGEDY*. Melpomene, the muse of tragedy. H: 6". She holds a knife and a goblet or bowl, in the manner of the classical figure of Melpomene made by Derby, circa 1753. Price A. © *Fitzwilliam Museum, Cambridge.*

Figure 183.4. *TRAGEDY, COMEDY.* The muses Melpomene and Thalia. H: ~6". Price B.

Figure 183.5. Melpomene, the muse of tragedy. H: ~6". Price A.

Figure 183.6. Thalia, the muse of comedy. H: ~6". Figures of Thalia and Melpomene in this style all appear to come from the same molds and may have emanated from the same pot bank. Price A.

Figure 183.7. Thalia, the muse of comedy. H: 6". Price A. *The William Herbert and Nancy Hunt Collection.*

184. Mercury

Mercury was the messenger of the gods. His attributes are all winged for speedy travel and include sandals, a hat, and a caduceus. His staff, entwined with two snakes, has magical powers. Only two examples of Mercury are recorded. One is impressed with John Dale's mark, and the other is attributed to the Brown Base Group. The figures are from the same molds, but the decoration and the addition of a bocage to the Dale figure suggest it postdates the Brown Base example.

Figure 184.1. Mercury. Attributed to Brown Base Group. H: 10". Price B.

Figure 184.2. Mercury; with bocage. Impressed "I. DALE BURSLEM". H: 10". Inscribed "mm" in ochre and "o" in green beneath the base. From the same molds as the previous figure. Price C. © *Christie's Images Limited 2014.*

185. Metis

Metis, Jupiter's first wife, was the goddess of deep thought and wisdom. When Metis was pregnant, Jupiter, fearing their child would be more powerful than he, turned Metis into a fly and swallowed her. Thus, their daughter Minerva emerged fully formed from Jupiter's head. Figures of Metis are known only from the examples shown here.

Figure 185.1. Metis. H: 14.7". Price C. *Collection of Arnold and Barbara Berlin.*

Figure 185.2. Metis. Attributed to Brown Base Group. H: 6.2". Price A.

186. Minerva

Minerva was the Roman goddess of wisdom. She was a war goddess who fought for just causes. Minerva was born from Jupiter's head and sprang forth fully armed. She is portrayed with an owl, denotative of her wisdom, and the owl is sometimes perched atop books to signify knowledge. Minerva's shield is decorated with Medusa's head because Minerva helped Perseus slay this gorgon. Derby figures of Minerva predate earthenware examples and may have inspired their creation.

Figure 186.1. *Minerva*. Attributed to Ralph Wood; impressed "53". H: 12.5". Price B. *Image courtesy of The Potteries Museum & Art Gallery, Stoke-on-Trent, UK.*

Figure 186.2. *Minerva*. Attributed to Ralph Wood; impressed "59". H: 11.7". Price B.

Figure 186.3. *Minerva*. Attributed to Ralph Wood. H: 12". Price B. © *Victoria and Albert Museum, London*.

Figure 186.4. Minerva. Attributed to Brown Base Group. H: 9.4". Price B.

Figure 186.5. Minerva. Possibly attributable to Brown Base Group or Lakin & Poole. H: 9.4". Pairs with Mars in figure 186.2. The rear of the base is not marbled, suggesting a Lakin linkage. Price B.

Figure 186.6. Minerva. Impressed "NEALE & Co". H: 8.1". Note the extensive gilding. Price B. *Image courtesy of The Potteries Museum & Art Gallery, Stoke-on-Trent, UK.*

Figure 186.7. Minerva. Probably made by the Leeds Pottery. H: 11". A very similar figure impressed "LEEDS POTTERY" is at Temple Newsam House (16.198/47). Price B. *Bonhams.*

187. Paris

In the myth of the Judgment of Paris, Paris awards a golden apple to Venus for triumphing over Juno and Minerva in a beauty contest. The tale has been represented in art since the sixth century B.C.E. William Congreve's *Judgment of Paris*, a popular satire in the guise of a classical myth, was first performed in London in 1701. It was staged at Covent Garden with modifications in 1759 and probably on provincial and fairground stages into the nineteenth century.

The figure of Paris below uses the same figure molds that Lakin & Poole used for Ganymede (chap. 173). Unlike Ganymede, Paris does not wear a Phrygian cap and he holds an apple. The example shown has no restoration to the hands. In other words, the figure is not an incorrectly restored example of Ganymede. The only other recorded example of Paris is in the Earle Collection (no. 451). That figure is on a delicately marbled base and pairs with a similarly styled Apollo in the collection (no. 455), both being in the manner of Lakin & Poole.

Figure 187.1. Paris. H: 13.1". Price B.

188. Peace

Peace is usually portrayed in figural form as a classically attired female, crowned with an laurel wreath and carrying an olive branch. From the Renaissance, art works have depicted Peace burning the weapons of war with her torch, and this portrayal is mirrored in most earthenware figures. Such figures are probably companion figures to similarly styled figures of Justice (chapter 178). Sometimes Peace is depicted holding a dove, but figures holding doves generally represent Venus (chap 194) or are allegorical portrayals of the element air (chap. 153). The putto shown in figure 188.4 is an unusual depiction of Peace known only from this example.

The large group in figure 188.6 symbolizes the hope for a peaceful resolution of the French Revolution. Here, implements of war on the base (helmets) and broken chains symbolize the fight for freedom. The male figure holds a shield decorated with the fleur-de-lys of the French monarchy. The female is offering him a Liberty bonnet. Clasped hands of fraternity are on the obelisk, so the group has been interpreted as suggesting a peaceful resolution of the French Revolution. That hope ended with the execution of Louis XVI in January 1793, so this group may have been made before that date.[1]

Figure 188.1. Peace. H: 8.3". "29" is painted within the body of the figure, which is open from beneath. Price A.

Figure 188.2. Peace. H: 8.6". A rare figure known only from this example. The facial features are contemporary rather than classical. Companion to Justice (fig. 178.2). Price B.

Figure 188.3. Peace. Attributed to Brown Base Group. H: 7.5". Price B.

Figure 188.4. Peace. Possibly made by Enoch Wood. H: 6". Base lost. Known from only this example. Forerunner to a Victorian putto allegorical of peace that pairs with another symbolizing war. These Victorian figures are associated with Thomas Parr, who re-used some of Enoch Wood's molds. Price A.

Figure 188.6. Group symbolic of a peaceful resolution of the French Revolution. H: 14". Price C.

Figure 188.5. Peace, reverse of previous figure.

189. Prometheus

Prometheus stole fire from the gods and gave it to mortals to improve their lives. As punishment, Jupiter ordered him chained to a rock where he was tortured daily by an eagle that dined on his liver. The motif shown here also appears on earthenware plaques, and it is thought to be derived from a design by Jean Voyez. It is first recorded on a basalt vase impressed with Humphrey Palmer's mark, and on the rock beneath Prometheus "J. Voyex, Sculpt 1769" is inscribed.[1]

Figure 189.1. Prometheus bound. H: 4.3". Formed with a flat, unpainted back. Price A. *Collection of Arnold and Barbara Berlin.*

190. Romulus and Remus

Roman mythology tells that in the eighth century B.C.E., the twins Romulus and Remus were born of the relationship between the god Mars and the vestal virgin Rhea Silvia. The twins were placed in a reed basket and abandoned, but a wolf suckled them. Romulus went on to found Rome. By legend, Romulus and Remus determined who would pick the city's site by contesting to determine who the better augur was. Romulus saw more vultures—indicating that the gods favored him—and vultures too are present on earthenware figure groups. Multiple pot banks made Romulus and Remus groups, but all are essentially the same in composition and appear to have been inspired by Peter Paul Rubens's seventeenth-century painting, or, more probably, a derivative print.

Figure 190.1. *Romulus and Remus*. Peter Paul Rubens, circa 1615.

Figure 190.2. *REMUS & ROMULUS*; with bocage. H: 7.8". Price B. *John Howard; www.antiquepottery.co.uk.*

Figure 190.3. *Romulus & Remus*; with bocage. H: ~7.3". Price B. *Andrew Dando Antiques.*

Figure 190.4. *Romulus & Remus*; with bocage. L: 7.8". Price A.

Figure 190.5. Romulus and Remus atop a watch stand. H: 11.8". The watch stand is made as one piece, open from beneath. Another example of the same form is recorded with a detachable lid. Price C. *Bearnes Hampton & Littlewood.*

Figure 190.6. Romulus and Remus atop a watch stand, reverse of previous example. Here a watch is integral to the design. *Bearnes Hampton & Littlewood.*

Figure 190.7. *REMUS & ROMULUS*; with bocage. Attributed to "Sherratt". H: ~8.5". Price C.

Figure 190.8. Romulus and Remus; with bocage. Attributed to "Sherratt". H: ~8.1". Bocage restored. On a lower (and possibly slightly earlier) base than the previous example. This group also occurs on a brown clawed base with two swags on the front apron. Price A.

Figure 190.9. Romulus and Remus; with bocage. Attributed to "Sherratt". H: 9". The splotched decoration of the base is as on the bocage trunks of some "Sherratt" figures. Price C. *The William Herbert and Nancy Hunt Collection.*

Figure 190.10. *REMUS & ROMULUS*; with bocage. H: 8.3". Price B. *Wisbech & Fenland Museum*.

Figure 190.11. *REMUS & ROMULUS*, reverse of previous example. John Walton and other potters used this bocage, but there is no basis for attributing this example to any particular pot bank. *Wisbech & Fenland Museum*.

Figure 190.12. *ROMULUS & REMUS*; with bocage. H: ~7". The titling is like that on the previous example but reversed. With remnants of five-leaflet bocage fronds, a form that occurs seldom on this group. Restorer's material evident. Price A.

Figure 190.13. Romulus and Remus; with bocage. H: ~8". With cilantro bocage fronds (with restored flowers) and apparently from a different pot bank to all previous examples on this theme. Price B.

191. Time

By the Renaissance, Father Time was represented with attributes that included wings and a snake circled with its tail in its mouth to symbolize eternity. The earthenware group of *Time Clipping the Wings of Love* is after an earlier Derby group after James Macardell's mezzotint of Anton Van Dyck's sixteenth-century painting. However, the figures are positioned differently in the earthenware group.

Figure 191.1. *Time Clipping the Wings of Love*, published by Carington Bowles circa 1766–1784, after James Macardell, after Anthony van Dyck.

Figure 191.2. *Time Clipping the Wings of Love*. Attributed to Lakin & Poole. H: 12.2". A marked example is in the Southport Museum, U.K. Price C.

Figure 191.3. Father Time. H: >18". Possibly the raised hand once held a scythe, hourglass, or some other attribute. Price B.

Figure 191.4. Father Time with a watch stand. H: 9". Price B. *Collection of Arnold and Barbara Berlin*.

192. Triton

The Greek god Triton was the son of Poseidon and Amphitrite, the god and goddess of the sea. Triton was the messenger of the deep, and he is usually represented as a merman. His attribute is a conch shell, which he blows to raise or calm the waves. Bronze-glazed tritons impressed "WOOD & CALDWELL" are recorded, and enamel-painted examples of these figures are traditionally attributed to Enoch Wood/Wood & Caldwell. The design source is a triton modeled for Wedgwood in 1769, after a sculpture by the architect William Chambers. By the 1770s, Derby had copied that figure.

Figure 192.1. Tritons, a pair. Probably made by Enoch Wood/Wood & Caldwell. H: ~9.3" max. A bronze-glazed pair (with conches of this height) is recorded. Price B. *Elinor Penna*.

Figure 192.2. Triton. Probably made by Enoch Wood/Wood & Caldwell. H: 9.9". The conch is taller than in the previous example. A triton to pair with this and holding a similarly tall conch to the other side is recorded. Price A. *Moylan-Smelkinson; The Spare Room*.

Figure 192.3. Triton. Probably made by Enoch Wood/Wood & Caldwell. H: 9.9". The base with ochre lines is typical of this pot bank. Price A. *www.madelena.com*.

193. Urania

Urania, the Greek goddess of truth, is also the muse of astronomy, and she is usually portrayed holding a globe or compass. In art, Urania is frequently depicted reclining against a globe with a compass in hand. In 1782, Johann Heinrich Tischbein the Elder painted her in this by-then traditional pose. The figure of Urania with a watch stand was probably influenced by some such art work. The standing figure of Urania derives from a similarly posed statue in the Vatican Museum. A reduced-scale plaster or bronze probably influenced its modeling.

Figure 193.1. *Urania*, by Crispijn de Passe the Elder (1590–1637).

Figure 193.2. Urania posed on a watch stand. H: 9.7". A similar example in the Earle Collection is titled on the front *THE GODDESS OF TRUTH*. Price C.

Figure 193.3. Roman marble of Urania, now in the Vatican.

Figure 193.4. *URANIA*. Attributed to Lakin & Poole. H: 11.8". The base and the style of titling are typical of this manufactory. Price B.

194. Venus and Neptune

Venus (the Roman goddess of love and the mother of Cupid) and Neptune (the god of the seas) are well represented in both ancient statuary and Old Master art works. By 1755, Derby had modeled Neptune posed, as in some earthenware figures, standing before a dolphin upon a shell encrusted mound, his raised arm holding a trident and his mantle billowing behind him. Venus may have been inspired by—but not copied from—Derby and Chelsea depictions of the same era. The dove is one of Venus's attributes, and some figures portray Venus with a dove. Such figures are sometimes interpreted as allegorical of the element air (chap. 153). Two figure groups, showing Venus playing with her son Cupid, are after Bow, Chelsea, and Derby groups of circa 1765 (figs. 194.40–41).

The Earle Collection records a most unusual example of Neptune (no. 168). It is described as "Neptune with trident in his right hand, at his feet two sea monsters, on each of which a boy is seated; decorated with representations of starfish, seaweed, etc. on circular moulded base with red lines". No other example of this group is known.

Figures 194.43–44 show two uncommon figures of Venus that are after Italy's marble Venus de Medici. For centuries, prints and statuary have captured the likeness of this first-century B.C.E. marble of a slender Venus, posed to conceal her nakedness. Ludwigsburg copied it in porcelain by circa 1765.[1] Later, the antique form was mimicked in enamel-painted earthenware, but modesty dictated concealing nudity.

Figure 194.1. *Venus, Neptune*. Attributed to Ralph Wood. H: ~9". These models occur impressed "21" (Venus) and "22" (Neptune). A different Ralph Wood model of Venus (holding a bird and without Cupid and a dolphin, figs. 194.34–35) pairs with Bacchus (fig. 162.3). Price B.

Figure 194.2. Neptune. H: 11".5". Companion subject to the following Venus. Price B. *Collection of Michael J. Smith*.

Figure 194.3. Venus. H: 11.4". Companion subject to the previous Neptune. Price B. *www.madelena.com*.

Figure 194.4. *VENUS*, (impressed twice on reverse of plinth) and Neptune. H: 10.3" (L), 11" (R). The lettering on *VENUS* is as found on Ralph Wedgwood figures, and possibly Wedgwood made this pair. Price C.

Figure 194.5. Neptune and Venus. H: 8.5" (L), 8.1" (R). Porcelainous/ stoneware bodies. A figure of Venus in the British Museum (AN965629001) with the base similarly decorated is painted "Absolon Yarm" (William Absolon of Yarmouth) beneath. Price B. © *Victoria and Albert Museum, London*.

Figure 194.6. Venus. Impressed "WEDGWOOD". H: 7.9". See figure 194.45 for another model of Venus also made by Wedgwood. Price A.

Figure 194.7. Neptune. H: 8.9". Price A. *M. J. Meehan.*

Figure 194.8. Neptune. H: ~9.1". Price A.

Figure 194.9. Neptune and Venus, an assembled pair. Possibly made by Enoch Wood. H: 9.4" (L), 8.7" (R). On Enoch Wood-type bases. A similar figure of Neptune was excavated from the Burslem Old Town Hall site associated with Enoch Wood circa 1820–1830, but other pot banks made comparable figures. Price A. *Brighton and Hove Museums.*

Figure 194.10. Neptune. Attributed to Brown Base Group. H: 8.4". Pairs with the following Venus. This model of Neptune also occurs on a base painted only with a line around it. Price B.

Figure 194.11. Venus. Attributed to Brown Base Group. H: 9.2". Pairs with the previous Neptune. Price B.

Figure 194.12. Venus. Probably made by Enoch Wood. H: ~9". The bocage (each frond has seven fern leaflets) and base are typical of Enoch Wood. Price A.

Figure 194.13. Neptune and Venus. Probably made by Enoch Wood. H: ~9.3" max. The bases and bocages (hawthorn leaves arranged in threes) are consistent with an Enoch Wood attribution. Price B.

Figure 194.14. Neptune and Venus. Possibly made by Enoch Wood. H: 7.5". Price B. *John Howard; www.antiquepottery.co.uk.*

Figure 194.15. Neptune. Possibly made by Enoch Wood. H: 7.4". Price A. *Brighton and Hove Museums.*

Figure 194.16. Neptune. Attributed to "Sherratt". H: ~9". Pairs with the following Venus. This rainbow base is specific to "Sherratt". Price D, pair. © *Victoria and Albert Museum, London.*

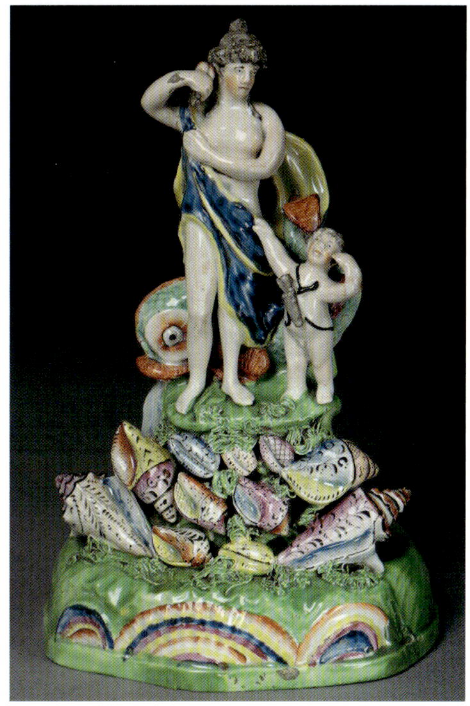

Figure 194.17. Venus. Attributed to "Sherratt". H: 9.5". Pairs with the previous Neptune. Price D, pair. © *Victoria and Albert Museum, London.*

Figure 194.18. *NEPTUNE &, VENUS*, a pair. Attributed to "Sherratt". H: 9.7" (left, excluding trident), 9.9" (R). "Sherratt" made Venus with two different heads. Her head here differs from the head on the previous and following "Sherratt" examples. Price D.

Figure 194.19. Neptune and Venus, reverse of previous pair. Price C.

Figure 194.20. Neptune, Venus, a pair. Attributed to "Sherratt". H: 9.7". Venus's head is restored. Price C.

Figure 194.21. Neptune. Attributed to "Sherratt". H: 9.3" (excluding trident). Companion to the following Venus. Price D, pair. *The William Herbert and Nancy Hunt Collection.*

Figure 194.22. Venus. Attributed to "Sherratt". H: ~9.5". Companion to the previous Neptune. Venus is also recorded titled on this base. Price D, pair. *The William Herbert and Nancy Hunt Collection.*

Figure 194.23. Neptune. Attributed to "Sherratt". H: 11.7" (excluding trident). Companion to the following Venus. Price D, pair. *The William Herbert and Nancy Hunt Collection.*

Figure 194.24. Venus. Attributed to "Sherratt". H: 11.5". Companion to the previous Neptune. Price D, pair. *The William Herbert and Nancy Hunt Collection.*

Figure 194.25. Venus, reverse of previous figure. On this figure and her companion Neptune, the backs of the mounds are shaped differently from those shown in fig. 194.19.*The William Herbert and Nancy Hunt Collection.*

Figure 194.26. Neptune. H: 8.3" (excluding trident). Note the unusual pink luster base. Price B. *Stair Galleries.*

Figure 194.27. Venus. Possibly made by the Leeds Pottery. H: 7.5". A figure from these molds at Temple Newsam House (16.207/47) is impressed "LEEDS POTTERY". Price A.

Figure 194.28. Venus. H: 7.4". Price A. *Elinor Penna.*

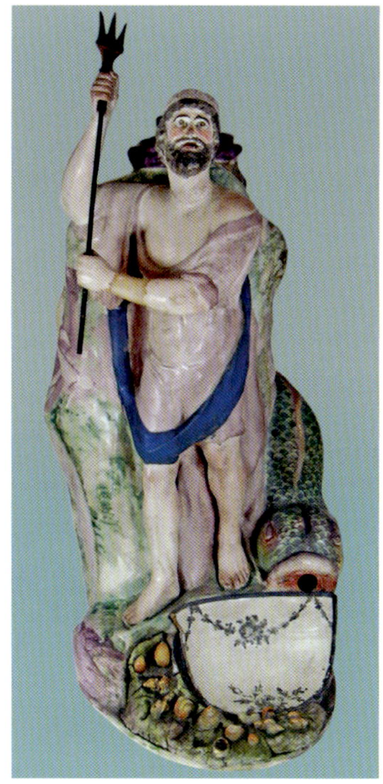

Figure 194.29. Neptune with a triton. H: 15.7". There are traces of gilding on his hat. A color-glazed example of this extraordinary figure is in the Fitzwilliam Museum (C.7–1933). Price C. *Brighton and Hove Museums.*

Figure 194.30. Neptune with a triton, reverse of previous figure. *Brighton and Hove Museums.*

Figure 194.31. Venus; with bocage. Attributed to Dale. H: ~7". The indentations and sprig on the base, the bocage leaves and flowers, and the plump facial features are typical of Dale. Companion to Bacchus (fig. 162.7). Price B.

Figure 194.32. Venus; with bocage. Attributed to Dale. H: ~7". Like the previous figure and with characteristic Dale sprigs on the base. Companion to Bacchus (fig. 162.7). Price B.

Figure 194.33. Venus. Impressed "WEDGWOOD". H: 29.4". A particularly large figure with impressive modelling and enameling. Price D. *Skinner, Inc.; www.skinnerinc.com.*

Figure 194.34. *Venus*. Attributed to Ralph Wood. H: ~9.2". Note Ralph Wood's different portrayal of Venus in figure 194.1. Price A. *M. J. Meehan.*

Figure 194.35. Venus. Attributed to Ralph Wood; impressed "57". H: 9.2". Price A.

Figure 194.36. Venus. Impressed "NEALE & Co". H: 8.7". Pairs with Bacchus (fig. 162.1). Price B. *Eileen and Robert Carde.*

Figure 194.37. Venus. H: 24.7". The large cherub in figure 197.12 is decorated similarly. Price C. *Collection of Arnold and Barbara Berlin.*

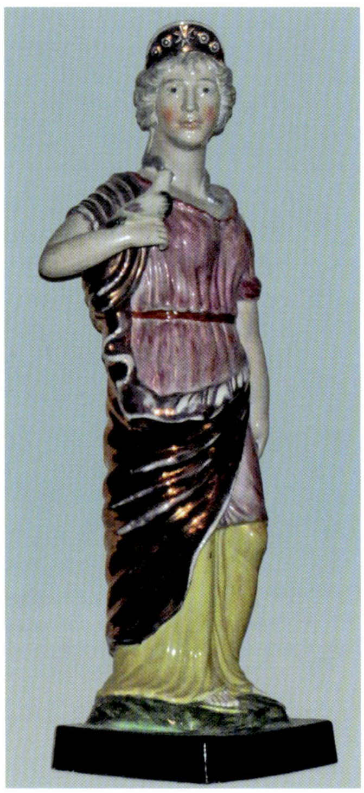

Figure 194.38. Venus. H: ~17". Price C. *Collection of Arnold and Barbara Berlin.*

Figure 194.39. Venus. H: 11". Price A. *Barbara Gair; www.castle-antiques.com.*

Figure 194.40. Venus playing with Cupid. Possibly made by Enoch Wood. H: 4.5". Companion to the following group. Both are after Bow, Chelsea, and Derby groups of circa 1765. Price A.

Figure 194.41. Venus playing with Cupid. Possibly made by Enoch Wood. H: 4.9". Price A.

Figure 194.42. *The Medici Venus*, Jan de Bisschop, 1669.

Figure 194.43. Venus de Medici. H: 24". Venus leans against a brown tree stump. The base is closed beneath, with a large ventilation hole beneath the support and a smaller one beneath the dolphin. An example from these molds is inscribed "THOMAS LEEK 1819".[2] Price C. © *Fitzwilliam Museum, Cambridge.*

Figure 194.44. Venus de Medici. H: 31". This is the largest figure recorded. Price C. *The Earle Collection, no. 408.*

Figure 194.45. *VENUS* (impressed on the front of the base). Impressed "WEDGWOOD". H: ~6.3". The titling (small, impressed letters like those used for the "WEDGWOOD" mark) is typical of Wedgwood. See figure 194.6 for another model of Venus also made by Wedgwood. Price A. *Image courtesy of The Potteries Museum & Art Gallery, Stoke-on-Trent, UK.*

195. Unidentified and Other Classical Figures

A 19.5-inch figure of a classically attired young girl holding her skirt with one hand and a flaming torch with the other is recorded, but it is not shown in this work. This figure is mounted on a round black-marbled base and is marked "WEDGWOOD & CO" (the mark of Ralph Wedgwood).

Also recorded, but not shown here, are a twenty-three inch figure of a slender youth, clad in only a fig leaf and possibly representing Adonis,[1] an eight-and-a-half-inch figure thought to be Adonis, with a cloth draped from his shoulder to cover his nudity and impressed WEDGWOOD,[2] and a five-inch figure of Actaeon impressed "NEALE & Co".[3] See figure 171.30 for a much cruder figure of Actaeon of the same form.

The figure group of *Roman Charity* (fig. 195.20) depicts a subject that has been popular in art for centuries and that is also portrayed in Grecian Daughter groups in Volume 2, chapter 40. First modeled by Ralph Wood circa 1790, it shows Pero, who breastfeeds her father Cimon after he has been sentenced to death by starvation. The group is usually decorated with colored glazes, and enamel-painted examples are uncommon.

Figure 195.1. A large classical group, with a lady giving alms to a beggar while a gentleman watches. H: 14.3", L: 12". The only recorded example. A helmet (perhaps symbolic of war) lies on the ground. Price D. *The William Herbert and Nancy Hunt Collection.*

Figure 195.2. Lady on a pedestal base. H: 9.3". Price B. *Andrew Dando Antiques.*

Figure 195.3. Man holding a pot. H: 7". Price A. *Robert Hawker.*

Figure 195.4. Lady holding a bow. H: 5.5", L: 5.5". The figure itself is flat and unpainted on the reverse. Pairs with the following figure. Price A. *The William Herbert and Nancy Hunt Collection.*

Figure 195.5. Lady seated with a sheaf of wheat. H: 5", L: 6.7". Pairs with the previous figure and is similarly flat and unpainted on the reverse. Price A. *The William Herbert and Nancy Hunt Collection.*

Figure 195.6. Lady seated with a sheaf of wheat. H: 5.1", L: 6.7". Like the previous figure but on a differently shaped base. The reverse of the figure form is again flat and unpainted. Price A.

Figure 195.7. A pair of figures, each with two maidens dancing; with bocages. H: 9.2". Price B.

Figure 195.8. Two figures of girls each holding a fish, formed as candlesticks with the candle holders atop the heads. H: ~9". Price C.

Figure 195.9. Classical lady, formed as a candlestick with the candle holder atop her head. H: 8". "43" painted in black beneath. Price B. © *Fitzwilliam Museum, Cambridge.*

Figure 195.10. *Fortune*. Impressed "W" and made by Ralph Wood. H: 11". From the same molds as Plenty (fig. 166.9) attributed to Ralph Wood but with the addition of the adornment atop her head. Price B.

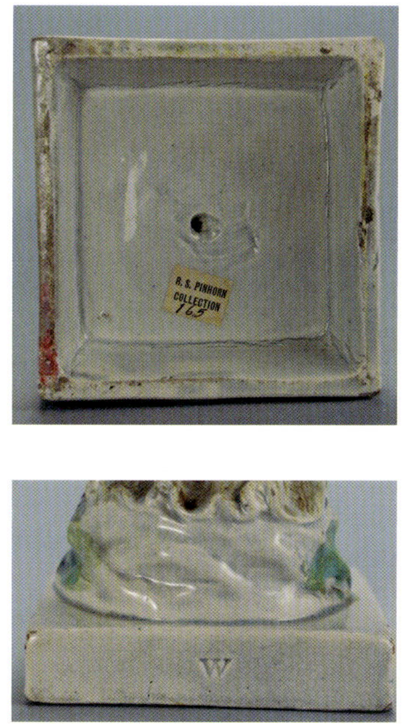

Figure 195.11. *Fortune,* detail of the previous figure. "W" is impressed on the back of the base. The interior of the base is atypical as the bases of Ralph Wood figures usually have rounded internal corners.

Figure 195.12. Classical lady, probably a muse (L) and Calliope (R), a pair. H: 12.7". Price B each. *The William Herbert and Nancy Hunt Collection.*

Figure 195.13. Classical lady holding a vase. H: 18". Her right hand once held a metal fitting. Price B.

Figure 195.14. Classical lady holding a vase, reverse of previous figure.

Figure 195.15. Classical lady. Attributed to Brown Base Group. H: 6". This is the smallest Brown Base Group figure recorded. Her left arm is lost. Price A. *Image courtesy of The Potteries Museum & Art Gallery, Stoke-on-Trent, UK.*

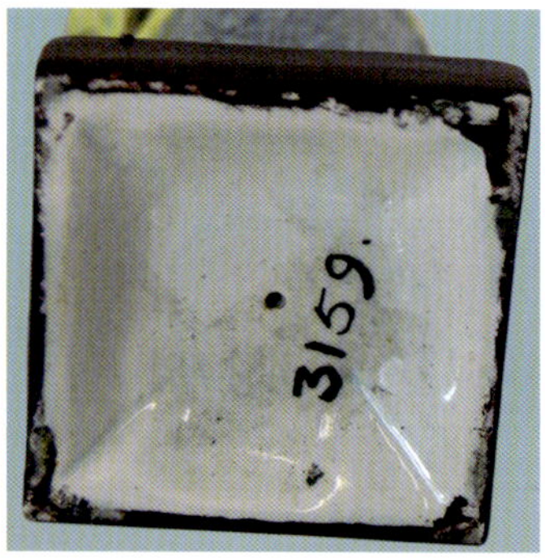

Figure 195.16. Base of previous figure. The internal corners are tooled in a manner typical of Brown Base Group figures.

Figure 195.17. Vulcan, the Roman god of fire. H: 8". Vulcan was a blacksmith who forged weapons for the gods. His awkward stance betrays a deformity resulting from Jupiter flinging him from Olympus in rage. This figure is known from only this example. Price A. *The William Herbert and Nancy Hunt Collection.*

Figure 195.18. Vulcan, reverse of previous figure. A figure emblematic of water with a similarly painted base has the mark of William Absolon of Yarmouth (fig. 153.10).*The William Herbert and Nancy Hunt Collection.*

Figure 195.19. Classical figure with a candle holder atop her head. H: ~8". Price A. *Elinor Penna*.

Figure 195.20. *ROMAN CHARITY* (impressed on side). H: 7.2". Portrays Pero with Cimon whom she breastfeeds when he is sentenced to death by starvation. Like the Ralph Wood color-glazed figure that can occur impressed "92" or "93". Price A. *The William Herbert and Nancy Hunt Collection.*

196. Chariots

The identity of the ladies in the largest earthenware chariot groups is uncertain (figs. 196.3–6). These groups echo contemporary prints depicting mythological and allegorical figures (including Plenty, Peace, Ceres, Pomona, Britannia, Africa, and America) seated in chariots pulled by felines. Some smaller earthenware chariot groups have Venus being pulled by cupids (figs. 196.7–10).

Figure 196.1. *Flora*. Reverse-painted print applied to glass. Published July, 1810.

Figure 196.2. *Ceres the Goddess of Plenty*. Reverse-painted print applied to glass. Published by W. B. Walker, circa 1800.

Figure 196.3. Chariot drawn by two tigers, a classical lady wearing a crown seated within; with bocage. Attributed to Dale. H: 10.5", L: 11". The base and bocage link to Dale, and her facial features are typical of Dale. Price G.

Figure 196.4. Chariot drawn by two lions, a classical lady with a tambourine within; with bocage. Attributed to Patriotic Group. L: 9.9". From the same molds as the following example but with cilantro bocage fronds. These lions occur as individual figures attributed to Patriotic Group. Price D. *Photograph Courtesy of Sotheby's, Inc. © 2014.*

Figure 196.5. Chariot drawn by two lions, a classical lady with a tambourine within; with bocage. Attributed to Patriotic Group. L: 10". The pinecone bocage is characteristic of the Group. Companion to the following chariot. Price D.

Figure 196.6. Chariot drawn by two leopards, a classical lady with a ewer and urn within; with bocage. L: 9.9". Attributed to Patriotic Group. Bocage restored. Companion to previous chariot. These leopards occur as individual figures attributed to Patriotic Group. Price C.

Figure 196.7. *VEANOUS AND CUPED ITS*. Venus in a chariot drawn by two cupids. Attributed to "Sherratt". H: 5.5", L: 6". Made without bocage. Price D. *The William Herbert and Nancy Hunt Collection.*

Figure 196.8. Venus in a chariot drawn by two cupids. Attributed to "Sherratt". H: ~5.5". Made without bocage. Like the previous example but the lady's head is different. Price C.

Figure 196.9. Venus in a chariot drawn by two cupids; with bocage. Attributed to "Sherratt". H: ~6". Like the previous examples but with a typical "Sherratt" bocage. The lady's head is as in figure 196.7. Price C.

Figure 196.10. Venus in a chariot drawn by two cupids. Attributed to Blue Group. H: 5.2". The flowers support the attribution. Price B.

Figure 196.11. Lady seated in a chariot drawn by an elephant. H: 4.3", L: 6.4". Made without bocage. Price B. *Collection of Arnold and Barbara Berlin*

Figure 196.12. Lady seated in a chariot drawn by a horse with rider. L: ~6". Made without bocage. Price A.

197. Cupids, Cherubs, and Putti

Figure 197.1. The struggle of Eros and Anteros. Impressed "WEDGWOOD & CO". H: 16.4". Cupid, known as Eros to the Greeks, struggles with Anteros, his brother. Modeled after a marble by Francois-Joseph Le Clercq, dated 1780, now in the Philbrook Museum of Art. Price D. © *Victoria and Albert Museum, London.*

Figure 197.2. The struggle of Eros and Anteros. H: 16.5". Unusual in that the wings are gilded. In keeping with the theme, one of the brothers is about to trample on a heart. Price C. *Elinor Penna.*

Figure 197.3. The struggle of Eros and Anteros. Impressed "WEDGWOOD". H: 16.4". Here the garland is placed to partially conceal nudity. Price D. *Angus Northeast.*

Figure 197.4. The struggle of Eros and Anteros. H: 17". Made without the garland draped across the body in previous examples, and a leaf conceals nudity. Price C. *Collection of Arnold and Barbara Berlin.*

Figure 197.5. The struggle of Eros and Anteros. Attributed to Enoch Wood/Wood & Caldwell. H: 16.2". Price C. *Elinor Penna.*

Figure 197.6. The struggle of Eros and Anteros, reverse of previous example. *Elinor Penna.*

Figure 197.7. The struggle of Eros and Anteros, detail of the previous example showing the four-petalled flowers that support the Wood/ Wood & Caldwell attribution. *Elinor Penna.*

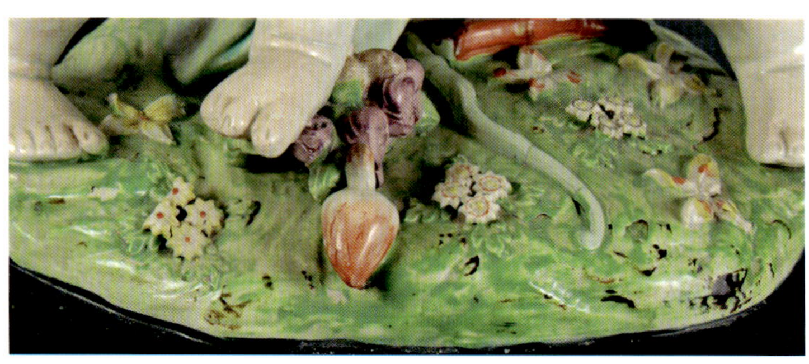

Figure 197.8. The struggle of Eros and Anteros; with bocage. H: 5.8". The heart in the foreground of this group is disproportionately large. These three-leaflet bocage fronds occur on a number of unclassified figures from the same pot bank. Price B. *Elinor Penna*.

Figure 197.9. Cupid with two small lions. H: 16.5". The large cupid towering over small lions may symbolize the power of love. Note the holes in each arm, perhaps to support a metal object of sorts. Also occurs with pink luster. Price C. *Collection of Arnold and Barbara Berlin*.

Figure 197.10. Cupid with two small lions. H: 16.6". This figure model is often attributed to Enoch Wood/Wood & Caldwell but an example with features supporting attribution has not been documented. It probably derives from a plaster after an il Fiammingo putto. Note the similar head on the bust in figure 200.145. Price B. *Elinor Penna*.

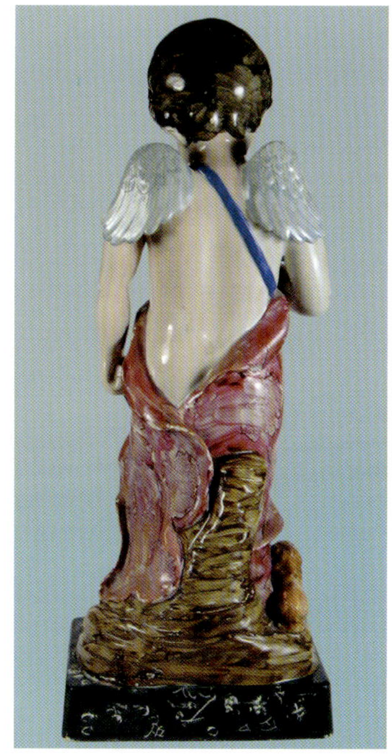

Figure 197.11. Cupid with two small lions, reverse of previous figure. *Elinor Penna*.

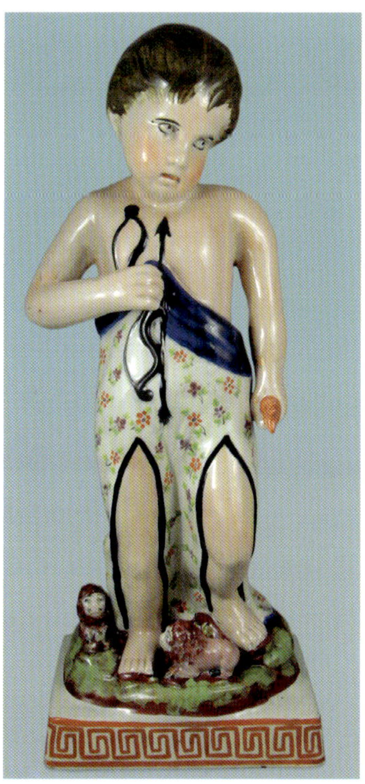

Figure 197.12. Cupid with two small lions. H: 17". Apparently painted by the same hand as figure. 194.37. Price B. *The William Herbert and Nancy Hunt Collection*.

Figure 197.13. *A CONSCRIPT*. H: 5.5". Cupid is portrayed being punished for his frequent mischief. He holds a naval hat on his shoulder. Price B.

Figure 197.14. Putto astride a barrel. Attributed to "Sherratt". Height unknown. Price B.

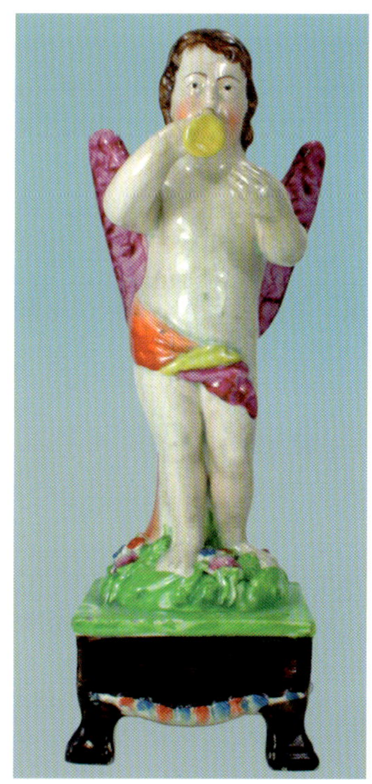

Figure 197.15. Putto representing the Archangel Gabriel. Attributed to "Sherratt". H: 9.3". A similar figure is titled *PREPARE TO MEET THY GOD* (Vol. 2, fig. 110.3). Price B. *Elinor Penna*.

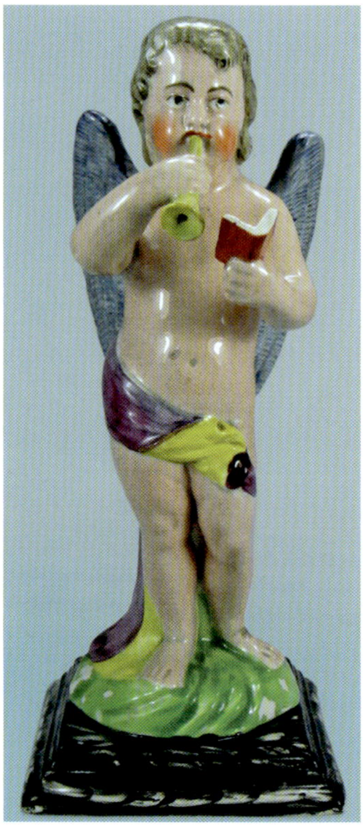

Figure 197.16. Putto representing the Archangel Gabriel. H: 7.7". Apparently uses the same figure molds as the previous and following figures but with no manufactory-specific features. Price B. *Elinor Penna*.

Figure 197.17. Cupid with a quiver. H: 8.7". Price B. *Elinor Penna*.

Figure 197.18. Putto holding a dove. H: 9.3". Wings restored. Price A.

Figure 197.19. Putto holding a dove. Possibly attributable to Patriotic Group. H: 6". The base suggests the attribution. Also noted is a similar figure on this base (clothing draped in the other direction) holding a sickle and wheat. Perhaps that figure represents summer and this represents spring. Price A.

Figure 197.20. Putto upon a column holding a dove. H: 7.1". The enamel colors suggest manufacture in the late eighteenth century. Price A.

Figure 197.21. Putto holding a dove; with bocage. H: ~4.5". After the previous model. Note the similarity to figure 155.107 titled *SUMMER*. Right side of the bocage restored. Price A.

Figure 197.22. Putto holding a basket; with bocage. Possibly made by Enoch Wood. H: 3.6". Price A.

Figure 197.23. Putto holding a basket on the left; with bocage. Probably made by Enoch Wood. H: ~4.5". Companion to the following figure. Price A.

Figure 197.24. Putto holding a basket on the right; with bocage. Attributed to Enoch Wood. H: ~4.5". Matches an excavated Enoch Wood figure of circa 1820–30 from the Burslem Old Town Hall site, now in the Fitzwilliam Museum (EC.35.2-1943). Companion to the previous figure. Price A.

Figure 197.25. Putti, a pair, each holding a basket to the side; with bocages (with restoration). Attributed to Enoch Wood. H: ~4.8". Like previous examples but with flowers on the bases. Price A.

Figure 197.26. Putti, a pair, each holding a basket to the side; with bocages. Probably made by Enoch Wood. H: 4.5". The bocages (one leaflet atop three) and the flowers on the base are typical of Enoch Wood. Similar putti impressed "32" beneath are recorded. Price A. *Andrew Dando Antiques.*

Figure 197.27. Putti, a pair, each holding a basket to the side; with bocages. H: 5". These three-leaflet bocage fronds occur on a number of unclassified figures from the same pot bank. Price A.

Figure 197.28. Putto holding a basket to the right; with bocage. H: ~5.2". The mound is unusual. Price A.

Figure 197.29. Putto holding a basket to the left; with bocage. Impressed "WALTON". H: ~5.8". Price A.

Figure 197.30. Putto holding a basket to the left; with bocage. Impressed "WALTON". H: 5.3". Similar to the previous putto but holding a different basket. Price A. *Peter Flemans*.

Figure 197.31. Putto holding a basket to the right; with bocage. Impressed "WALTON". H: 5.5". On the same base as the previous putto and possibly a companion. Price A. *Peter Flemans*.

Figure 197.32. Putti, a pair, each holding a basket; with bocages. Impressed "WALTON". H: 5.5". With different heads from previous Walton putti and on different bases. Price B. *Peter Flemans*.

Figure 197.33. Putto holding a basket to the left; with bocage. Impressed "WALTON". H: 5.5". On the same base as previous figures, but the putto's head may be from different molds. The eyebrows have eyelashes painted above them and are atypical of Walton's decorative style. Price A. *Peter Flemans*.

Figure 197.34. Putto, reverse of previous figure. Marked in the same manner as other putti shown here. *Peter Flemans*

Figure 197.35. Putto holding a basket; with bocage. Impressed "WALTON". H: ~3.7". Putti like this are the only marked Walton figures with this particular bocage form. Price A.

Figure 197.36. Putto holding a basket; with bocage. H: 4.2". Price A. *Andrew Dando Antiques.*

Figure 197.37. Putto holding a basket; with bocage. H: ~3.7". Price A.

Figure 197.38. Putto holding a basket; with bocage. H: 3.8". Price A.

Figure 197.39. Putto holding a basket; with bocage. H: 4". Price A.

Figure 197.40. Putto holding a basket; with bocage. H: ~4.5". Price A.

Figure 197.41. Putto holding a basket; with bocage. Attributed to Patriotic Group. H: ~4.4". The sprig atop the basket is specific to Patriotic Group. The same bocage and base are seen on figure 30.57 (Vol. 1). Price A.

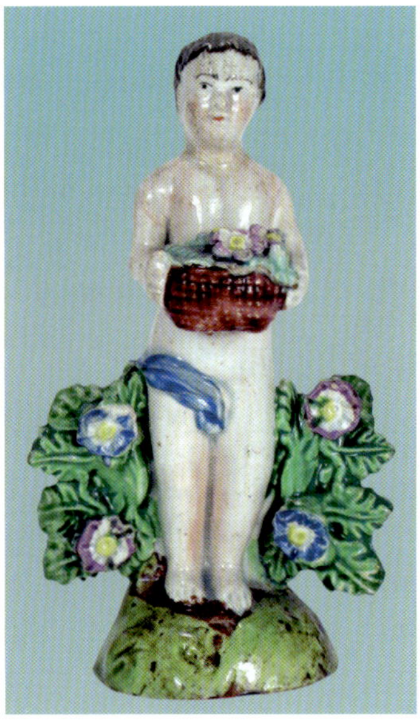

Figure 197.42. Putto holding a basket; with bocage. H: ~ 4.4". Price A.

Figure 197.43. Putto holding a basket; with bocage. H: 4.4". Price A. *Collection of Arnold and Barbara Berlin.*

Figure 197.44. Pair of putti holding baskets; with bocages. H: ~4.4". Price A.

Figure 197.45. Putto holding a basket; with bocage. Possibly made by "Sherratt". H: ~4.6". The base with leaf sprigs molded into it is typical of "Sherratt". Price A.

Figure 197.46. Putto holding a basket. Possibly made by "Sherratt". H: ~4.5". Made without bocage. The sprigging molded into the base occurs on other small figures attributed to "Sherratt". Price A.

Figure 197.47. Boy with basket; with bocage. Impressed "EDGE & GROCOTT". H: 5.3". This base form only occurs on the handful of known Edge & Grocott figures. Price B.

Figure 197.48. *BASKET BOY*; with bocage. Attributed to Blue Group. H: 5.3". The distinctive modeling of the bocage leaves establishes the attribution.

Figure 197.49. *BASKET BOY*, detail of reverse of a bocage leaf on previous figure. Two stubby flower stalks (yellow arrows) and two tiny leaves (red arrows) are added to the mid-line of an otherwise conventional seven-leaflet fern frond. This treatment is specific to Blue Group. Price A. *Andrew Dando Antiques.*

Figure 197.50. *BASKET BOY*; with bocage. Attributed to Blue Group. H: 5.3". Companion to the previous figure, having the same modified fern leaf fronds that are characteristic of this Group. Price A.

Figure 197.51. Putto holding a basket; with bocage. Attributed to Patriotic Group. H: ~5.9". The bocage flowers support the attribution. Price A.

Figure 197.52. Putto holding a basket; with bocage. Attributed to Patriotic Group. H: ~5". The floral sprigs atop each basket support the attribution, and the base and bocage are typical. Price A.

Figure 197.53. Putto holding a basket; with bocage. H: ~5.5". The painting is typical of the Blue Group, but the cupped bocage leaves and the flowers are atypical. Similarities to the following putto (especially the head, basket, and base) suggest the figures may be from the same pot bank. Price A.

Figure 197.54. Putto holding a basket; with bocage. H: ~5". From the same molds and with the same garment pattern as the putto on the left in figure 197.55. Both examples are from the same pot bank, as are other unclassified figures with these tiny five-petalled bocage flowers. Price A.

Figure 197.55. Two putti, each holding a basket, with a lamb; with bocage. H: ~7". From the same pot bank as the previous putto. Both examples have flower forms associated with an as yet unclassified Group of figures. Also see figure 203.3 from the same pot bank. Price B.

Figure 197.56. Putti, a pair, each holding a kaleidoscope; with bocages. Attributed to "Sherratt". H: ~6.2". Right, bocage restored. Price B.

Figure 197.57. Putto leaning right and holding a kaleidoscope; with bocage. Attributed to "Sherratt". H: 6.1". The small object in the hand touching the base appears to be a magnifying glass. This object occurs only on "Sherratt" putti leaning right, and, if not painted distinctively, is indistinguishable from the base. Price A.

Figure 197.58. Putto leaning left and holding a kaleidoscope; with bocage. Attributed to "Sherratt". H: ~6.3". Price A.

Figure 197.59. Putto leaning right and holding a kaleidoscope; with bocage. Attributed to "Sherratt". H: 6.3". Unlike the previous examples, the putto does not wear a leaf to conceal his nudity. The small object in the hand on the base is picked out in red, making it more visible than usual. Price B.

Figure 197.60. Detail of the front and back of the "Sherratt" bocage on the previous figure. This bocage often occurs with figures decorated in a turquoise palette.

Figure 197.61. Putto leaning right and holding a kaleidoscope; with bocage. Attributed to "Sherratt". H: ~5.7". Bocage restored. Price A.

Figure 197.62. Putto leaning right and holding a kaleidoscope; with bocage. Attributed to "Sherratt". H: ~6.8". Bocage restored. Price A.

Figure 197.63. Putto leaning left and holding a kaleidoscope; with bocage. Attributed to "Sherratt". H: ~6.3". Price A.

Figure 197.64. Putto holding a kaleidoscope; with bocage. Attributed to Hall. H: ~6". These star-shaped bocage flowers are characteristic of Hall. Price A.

Figure 197.65. Putto holding a kaleidoscope; with bocage. Probably made by Hall. H: ~6". The oak-leaf bocage with acorns, when made in this way, strongly suggests a Hall attribution. Price A.

Figure 197.66. Putto facing left and holding a kaleidoscope; with bocage. Probably made by Hall. H: ~6". Like the previous putti. Red and blue carnations are typical of Hall, as is the manner in which the fronds are fashioned. Price A.

Figure 197.67. Putto holding a kaleidoscope; with bocage. H: ~6". Unlike all previous putti and lacking characteristics to suggest attribution. Price A.

Figure 197.68. Inkstand formed as a putto astride a dolphin. H: ~5.5". An example in the Fitzwilliam Museum (c.981-1911) is inscribed "John Forster Made this Hanley Agust the 29 1820". The Fitzwilliam putto wears a hat, as does the putto in a similar inkstand in the Earle Collection (no. 664). Price A. *Aurea Carter Antiques.*

Figure 197.69. Inkstand formed as a putto astride a dolphin. H: 5.5". Unlike other examples, the putto has wings and the quiver is placed between the wings. On such inkstands, the quiver serves as a penholder, and the shell holds the ink. Price A. The Potteries Museum.

Figure 197.70. Inkstand formed as a putto astride a dolphin, reverse of previous example. *Image courtesy of The Potteries Museum & Art Gallery, Stoke-on-Trent, UK.*

Figure 197.71. Inkstand formed as a putto astride a dolphin. H: 5.7". The putto has a longer neck than in previous examples and was made without wings. Price A. *Image courtesy of The Potteries Museum & Art Gallery, Stoke-on-Trent, UK.*

Figure 197.72. Inkstand with putto astride a dolphin. H: 5". Made without wings and with the addition of shells to the corners of the base. Price A. *Martyn Edgell Antiques Ltd.*

Figure 197.73. Pair of putti, each slumbering upon a cushion with a basket of fruit and flowers. L: ~5" each. Price B. *John Howard; www.antiquepottery.co.uk.*

Figure 197.74. Putto, to the left, slumbering upon a cushion with a basket of fruit and flowers. H: 2.8", L: 5". Unusual in that the putto is black. Price A. *Collection of Arnold and Barbara Berlin.*

Figure 197.75. Putto, to the right, slumbering, with a basket of fruit and flowers. L: ~4.5". The marbling on the base is painted in a manner suggestive of "Sherratt". Price A.

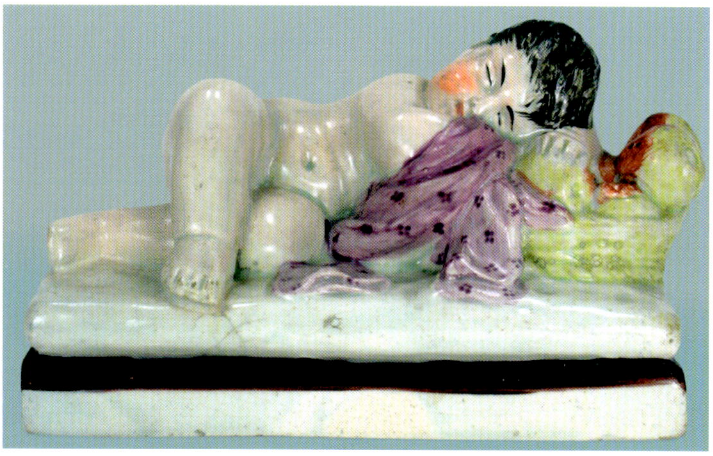

Figure 197.76. Putto, to the right, slumbering, with a basket of fruit. Impressed "WEDGWOOD". L: 4.3". Price A.

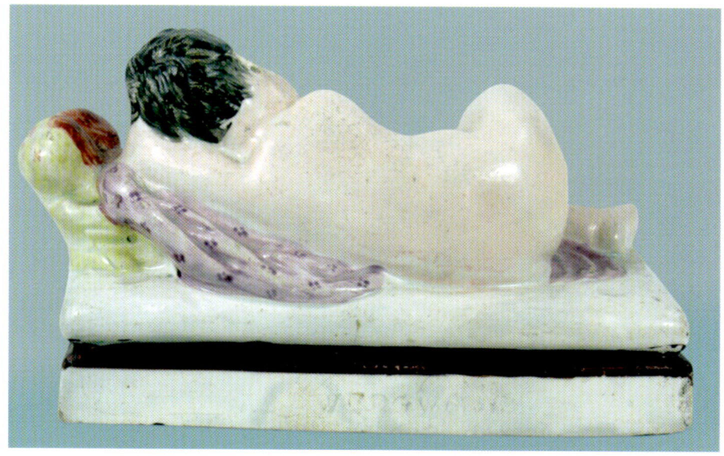

Figure 197.77. Putto, reverse of previous figure. "WEDGWOOD" is faintly impressed along the back of the base.

Figure 197.78. Pair of recumbent putti, one holding a bird. Both impressed "WEDGWOOD". L: 9.1". Price A. *Skinner, Inc.; www.skinnerinc.com.*

Figure 197.79. Putto slumbering, with four squirrels; with spill vase. H: 8.4". Spill vases of this form occur with animal subjects and all are probably from the same pot bank (Vol. 3, figs. 119. 79–80, 123.7, 126.136–137, 131.94–95). Price B. *Collection of Arnold and Barbara Berlin.*

Figure 197.80. Two putti playing. H: 4.5". Possibly representing Eros and Anteros at play. The figure is flat and unpainted on the back. The same motif is on the dovecote in Volume 3, figure 113.1. Price A.

Figure 197.81. Putto playing a pipe alongside a putto holding flowers. H: ~4". The figure is flat and unpainted on the back. The same motif is on the dovecote in Volume 3, figure 113.1. Price A. *Collection of Barbara Hunt Crow.*

Figure 197.82. Putto bound to a rock. H: 5", L: 6". Probably a representation of Cupid being punished for a mischievous deed. The motif is flat and unpainted on the back. A similar example on a brown base is recorded. Price A. *Collection of Arnold and Barbara Berlin.*

Figure 197.83. Pair of putti, each with a vase shaped as a cornucopia. H: 9.4". Price B. *Aurea Carter Antiques.*

Figure 197.84. Putto with a vase shaped as a cornucopia. H: 9". Price A. K. Stafford.

Figure 197.85. Putto or youth holding a cup. Impressed "WOOD & CALDWELL". H: 8.5". Price A. *M. J. Meehan.*

Figure 197.86. Putto or youth holding a cup. Impressed "WOOD & CALDWELL". H: 8.5". Price A.

Figure 197.87. Pair of putti or youths, each holding a cup. Attributed to Wood & Caldwell. H: 7.8". The cups lack bases, so perhaps they were intended to hold a spill or some other slender object. Price B. *The William Herbert and Nancy Hunt Collection.*

Figure 197.88. Putto reading, with a candlestick. Probably made by Wood & Caldwell/Enoch Wood. H: 6.9". This figure occurs impressed "WOOD & CALDWELL" (Temple Newsam House 28/37/41). Price A. *Image courtesy of The Potteries Museum & Art Gallery, Stoke-on-Trent, UK.*

Figure 197.89. Putti reading, a pair, with candlesticks. Probably made by Wood & Caldwell/Enoch Wood. H: 7". Price A. *Collection of Arnold and Barbara Berlin.*

Figure 197.90. Candlestick modeled as a female putto. H: 9.1". Price A. *Aurea Carter Antiques.*

Figure 197.91. Candlestick modeled as a putto. H: 8.7". A fluted sconce may have sat atop this candlestick. Price A. *Collection of Arnold and Barbara Berlin*

Figure 197.92. Pair of putti, each formed as a candlestick. H: 10.6". Price B. *Bonhams.*

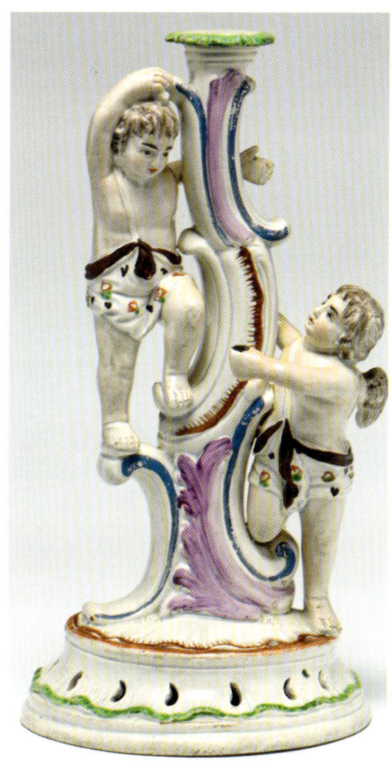

Figure 197.93. Pair of putti clambering up a candlestick. Impressed "T. Smith". H: 8.5". Figures by this maker are rare, and no other example of this candlestick, marked or unmarked, is recorded. Price B. © *Fitzwilliam Museum, Cambridge.*

198. People Resting on Plinths[1]

Figure 198.1. Girl kneeling against a plinth, to the right. H: ~2.5". The girl's eyes are closed. Price A.

Figure 198.2. Girl kneeling against a plinth, to the right. H: ~2.5". The girl's eyes are open. Price A.

Figure 198.3. Girl kneeling against a plinth, to the right. Attributed to "Sherratt". H: 2.4", L: 3.9". Pairs with the following figure. The floral sprigs applied to the base are specific to "Sherratt". As in all the following "Sherratt" figures, the girl's eyes are closed. Price A.

Figure 198.4. Girl kneeling against a plinth, to the left. Attributed to "Sherratt". H: ~2.4", L: ~3.9. Pairs with the previous figure. Price A.

Figure 198.5. Girl kneeling against a plinth, to the left. Attributed to "Sherratt". H: ~2.4", L: ~3.9". Price A.

Figure 198.6. Girl kneeling against a plinth, to the right. H: 2.5". Companion to the following figure. Price A. *Collection of Arnold and Barbara Berlin.*

Figure 198.7. Girl kneeling against a plinth, to the left. H: 2.6", L: 2.6". Companion to the previous figure. In both, the girl's eyes are open. Price A. *Mary and Maurice Norton.*

Figure 198.8. Box with girl kneeling against a plinth atop the lid. Attributed to "Sherratt". H: 5.3", L: 3.7". A similar box has a dog atop (Vol. 3, fig. 120.85). "Sherratt" features include the leafy sprigs, the wood-grain painting, and the coat of arms with the Prince of Wales's feathers (also on fig. 200.70). Price C. *Brighton and Hove Museums.*

Figure 198.9. Box with girl kneeling against a plinth atop the lid. Attributed to "Sherratt". H: 6", L: 5". Like the previous box but larger. The leafy sprigs on the front are as those on the aprons of some "Sherratt" table bases. Price C. *Doyle New York.*

Figure 198.10. Girl and boy, each holding a flower and leaning against a plinth; with bocage. H: 7.5". These three-leaflet bocage fronds occur on other unclassified figures from the same pot bank. Price B. *Elinor Penna.*

Figure 198.11. Girl and boy, each holding a flower and leaning against a plinth, reverse of previous example. *Elinor Penna.*

Figure 198.12. Base of previous example. *Elinor Penna.*

Figure 198.13. Girl and boy, each holding a flower and leaning against a plinth; with bocage. H: 7.5". Like the previous example, but the bocage fronds have five leaflets. Price B. *Collection of Michael J. Smith.*

Figure 198.14. Girl and boy, each holding a flower and leaning against a plinth; with bocage. H: ~6.4". Like previous examples but with yet another bocage form. Price A.

Figure 198.15. Girl and boy, she holding a flower, both leaning against a plinth; with bocage. H: ~5.4". Like previous examples but with the remnants of a bocage that appears to be of the form Ralph Wood used. Price A.

Figure 198.16. Girl and boy, each leaning against a plinth; with bocage. H: ~6.4". The bocage (with integral flowers) is molded as one piece and is unlike other recorded examples. Possibly flowers were once positioned in each raised hand. Price A.

Figure 198.17. Girl and boy, each holding a flower and leaning against a plinth, with restored bocage. H: ~7.5". Unlike other examples shown, this group is on an octagonal base. The motif on the plinth too differs. Price A.

Figure 198.18. Watch stand with a boy and girl to each side of a plinth, a cockerel atop. H: 10". The painted flower on the plinth and the children's raised arms are not seen on any of the following examples. Price A. *Woolley and Wallis Salisbury Salerooms Ltd.*

Figure 198.19. Watch stand with foliage, a boy and girl each holding a flower to either side of the plinth. H: 9". The central support for the watch holder is broader than on the following examples, and the leaves and flowers are unusual in form. Price C. *John Howard; www.antiquepottery.co.uk.*

Figure 198.20. Watch stand surrounded by foliage with birds, a boy and girl to each side of the plinth. H: 10.3". These three-leaflet fronds routinely occur on unclassified figures that tend to be finely enameled. Price C. *John Howard; www.antiquepottery.co.uk.*

Figure 198.21. Watch stand surrounded by foliage, a boy and girl to each side of the plinth. H: ~9". Like the previous example but lacking a bird, and the watch holder is formed differently. Price B.

Figure 198.22. Watch stand surrounded by foliage, a boy and girl to each side of the plinth, a bird atop. H: ~9". Like previous examples but with uncommon leaves. A watch is placed in the stand. Price C.

Figure 198.23. Watch stand with foliage with birds, a boy and girl to each side of the plinth. H: 8". The boy and girl each hold a flower. The bocage fronds have five leaflets. Price A. *Martyn Edgell Antiques Ltd.*

Figure 198.24. Watch stand formed as clock, flanked by a boy and a girl each leaning upon a plinth, he holds a flower. H: 10.8". Like the following example but not necessarily from the same pot bank. Such watch stands occur most commonly in under-glaze colors. Price A. *Barbara Gair, www.castle-antiques.com.*

Figure 198.25. Watch stand formed as clock, flanked by a boy and girl each leaning upon a plinth, he holds a flower. Impressed "DIXON, AUSTIN, & Co". H: 10.9". The mark is impressed onto the front lip, and holes to either side facilitate screwing the stand to a wooden surface. Note the extravagant use of pink luster. Price C.

Figure 198.26. Two vases, each upon a plinth flanked by a boy and girl, all mounted on a rocky base with sheep and a goat. Possibly made by Neale & Co. H: 12". A similar vase is impressed "NEALE & Co".[1] Comparable vases occur decorated in colored glazes. Price B, each. © *Fitzwilliam Museum, Cambridge.*

Figure 198.27. Vase upon a plinth flanked by a boy and girl. H: 9.1". Price A. *Elinor Penna.*

Figure 198.28. Base of previous example. *Elinor Penna.*

199. Miscellaneous Subjects

Figure 199.1. *I BULL* (impressed on front edge). A rotund man with a slab of meat and ale. H: 5". John Bull is the personification of the Englishman. Price A.

Figure 199.2. Rotund man with a slab of meat and ale, portraying John Bull. H: ~5". Price A. *John Howard; www.antiquepottery.co.uk.*

Figure 199.3. Rotund man with a slab of meat and ale, portraying John Bull. H: ~5". Price A.

Figure 199.4. Small toper on a beer barrel. H: 4.5". Price A.

Figure 199.5. Gentleman with food and ale, formed as a pepper pot. H: 4". Price A. *Image courtesy of The Potteries Museum & Art Gallery, Stoke-on-Trent, UK.*

Figure 199.6. Scotsman drinking. Made by the Scottish east coast potteries. H: 8.8". Figures on this base are thought to have been made at Thomas Rathbone's pot bank. Price B. *Andrew Dando Antiques.*

Figure 199.7. Gentleman. H: 5.7". Price A. *Andrew Dando Antiques.*

Figure 199.8. Gentleman. H: 4.8". Price A. *Peter Flemans.*

Figure 199.9. Gentleman; with bocage. H: ~5". Price A.

Figure 199.10. Gentleman; with bocage. H: ~5". Price A.

Figure 199.11. Scotsman wearing a kilt. H: 3.9". Like the following figure but made without a square base. Price A. *Kevin Stafford.*

Figure 199.12. Scotsman wearing a kilt. H: 4.3". Price A. *Whitehall Antiques, Chapel Hill, North Carolina.*

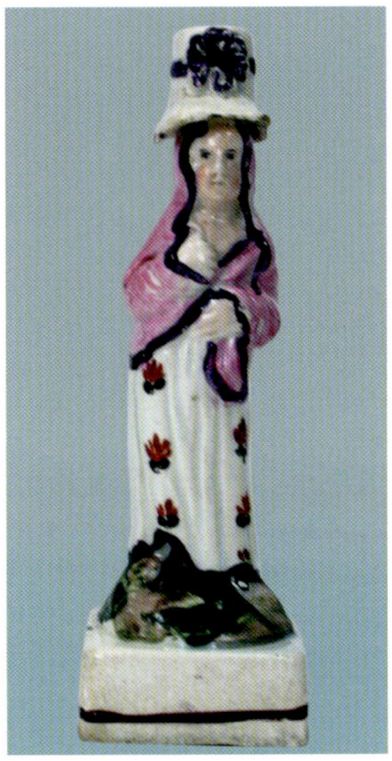

Figure 199.13. Lady with a flamboyant bonnet. H: 5.2". "3" is painted on the back edge of the base, above the painted line. Price A.

Figure 199.14. Lady holding a stick and a fan. H: ~5.3". Price A.

Figure 199.15. Seated gentleman holding a stick. H: 4.7". The figure pairs with a seated lady holding a bird. Price A. *Nick Burton.*

Figure 199.16. Bluecoat school boy. H: 3.8". Attired in a long blue coat and yellow socks, the traditional uniform established in Tudor times. Price A.

Figure 199.17. Lady; with bocage. Probably attributable to Patriotic Group. H: ~7.5". A similarly formed Patriotic Group figure (Vol. 2, fig. 84.11) portrays an archer. Here the bocage is consistent with a Patriotic Group attribution. Price A.

Figure 199.18. Gentleman. H: 9.6". His arm is lost. This model also portray a shepherd (Vol. 1, fig. 27.130) and the highwayman Jack Sheppard (Vol. 2, fig. 59.1). Price A. *Image courtesy of The Potteries Museum & Art Gallery, Stoke-on-Trent, UK.*

Figure 199.19. *Sloth*. Boy; with bocage. Attributed to Ralph Wood. H: 8.8". This figure form was first manufactured to represent *Winter* by Lunéville, after a model by Paul Louis Cyfflé. Ralph Wood examples occur impressed "5", "6", or "74" and may be untitled or titled *Sloth* or *Clown*. Price A. *Elinor Penna.*

Figure 199.20. Lady and gentleman dressed in late eighteenth-century attire, a pair; with bocages. H: 9.2". Both have lost their bases. Price B. *Brighton and Hove Museums*.

Figure 199.21. Lady. Impressed "LEEDS POTTERY". H: ~8". Traces of gilding are on her skirt. Her dress is similar in style to that on the lady in figure 199.20. Price B.

Figure 199.22. Child collecting shells; with bocage. H: 6". Potters who lived inland probably thought shells grew on the weird seaweed-like shrub that forms this bocage. Price B.

Figure 199.23. Child collecting shells; with bocage. H: 6". An example of such a group without the child but with two large birds is recorded (Vol. 3, fig. 113.74). Price B.

Figure 199.24. Child collecting shells; with bocage. H: 6". Price B.

Figure 199.25. Man and lady with dog, with arc bocage. H: ~6.9". Bases with this shield design are documented on figures of the Flight to Egypt, Return from Egypt, and a pair of standing lions. Price A.

Figure 199.26. Man seated; with bocage. Attributed to "Sherratt. H: 4.5". The bocage, base, and applied floral sprigs are all typical of "Sherratt". Price A.

Figure 199.27. Gentleman, lady with dog. Possibly by "Sherratt". H: 2.8" (L), 2.9" (R). The design integral to the bases of these diminutive figures is very suggestive of "Sherratt". Price A each. *www.madelena.com*.

Figure 199.28. Lady, two similar examples. H: 2.8" max. Such tiny figures are rare, and collectors treasure them. Price A each.

Figure 199.29. Gentleman and lady, an assembled pair. H: 2.9" max. An anchor is at her side, so she may symbolize Hope. Price A each.

Figure 199.30. Gentleman. H: 2.6". Price A. *K. Stafford.*

Figure 199.31. Lady; with bocage. Possibly made by "Sherratt". H: ~2.5". The bocage leaves suggest a "Sherratt" attribution. Price A.

Figure 199.32. Lady; with bocage. Possibly made by "Sherratt". H: ~2.5". The same figure as the previous example but with a different bocage that is not inconsistent with a "Sherratt" attribution. Price A.

Figure 199.33. Two naked babes; with bocage. Possibly made by "Sherratt". H: ~2.5". The bocage with these flowers occurs on "Sherratt" figures. Price A.

Figure 199.34. Two naked babes; with bocage. Possibly made by "Sherratt". H: ~2.5". Like the previous example and with a bocage suggestive of "Sherratt". Price A.

Figure 199.35. Lady resting. H: ~4". Price A.

Figure 199.36. Pair of topers, each seated upon a barrel, he with a glass in hand. H: 7.2". Price B. *Andrew Dando Antiques.*

Figure 199.37. Highlander holding a drinking horn. Probably made in Scotland by Thomas Rathbone & Co. H: 12.5". The Scottish east coast potteries' figures can be quite distinctive, and Rathbone was known for modeling figures after local characters. With both enamel and under-glaze colors. Price D. *Jonathan Horne.*

Figure 199.38. An actor or possibly a dandy gentleman. H: 8.5". With both enamel and under-glaze colors in a palette suggestive of the Scottish east coast potteries. Price B. *John Howard; www.antiquepottery.co.uk.*

Figure 199.39. A couple, perhaps Prince Leopold of Saxe-Coburg and Louise Marie of Orleans. H: 10". A transitional figure from the late 1830s. The decoration is typical of "Sherratt," but there is insufficient evidence for attribution. Price B. *The William Herbert and Nancy Hunt Collection.*

Figure 199.40. *A. Galego*. Lady water carrier. Attributed to Ralph Wood. H: ~9.5". A similar color-glazed figure bears Ralph Wood's mark, and another is impressed "67". Other Ralph Wood figures with a Spanish theme (*Spanish Dancers, Spanish Shepherd*) have impressed numbers in the upper 60s and low 70s. Price B. *Andrew Dando Antiques.*

Figure 199.41. *Mate*. Attributed to Dudson. H: ~10". Pairs with the Dudson *Gasconian* (Vol. 1, fig. 26.190), and these figures' large cloaks are a peculiar and attractive Dudson feature. Modeled after the previous Ralph Wood *A Galego*. Price A. *Andrew Dando Antiques.*

Figure 199.42. Classical lady with perhaps a crown atop her head. H: 5.3". Price A. Bamfords Auctioneers and Valuers Ltd.

Figure 199.43. Lady with an object atop her head. H: 11". Price B. *The William Herbert and Nancy Hunt Collection.*

Figure 199.44. Watch stand, with men flanking the columns and with cherubs atop. H: 8.3". "Sherratt" made these men as individual figures (Vol. 1, fig. 25.52, and Vol. 2, figs. 79.35–36) and included them on *PREPARE TO MEET THY GOD* groups representing tyler masons (Vol. 2, chap. 110). Other rare watch stands share similarities with this example Vol. 3, figs. 126.142–144, and fig. 199.45). Price C.

Figure 199.45. Watch stand, two tyler masons flanking a bee hive. H: 13.5". A possibly unique group symbolic of freemasonry. The tyler mason on the left is very similar to that on the previous watch stand and on *PREPARE TO MEET THY GOD* groups (chapter 110). Price D. *The William Herbert and Nancy Hunt Collection.*

Figure 199.46. Detail of the previous watch stand. The tyler masons flank a bee hive. Freemasons are proponents of industry, and the bee hive symbolizes this virtue. *The William Herbert and Nancy Hunt Collection.*

Figure 199.47. Reverse of the previous watch stand. The watch is fitted to the stand. *The William Herbert and Nancy Hunt Collection.*

Figure 199.48. *JOHN BULL*. Figural pipe depicting John Bull. H: 5.5". John Bull is the personification of the Englishman. Price B. *Image courtesy of The Potteries Museum & Art Gallery, Stoke-on-Trent, UK.*

Figure 199.49. Figural pipe depicting a lady wearing a top hat. H: 6.3". Price B.

Figure 199.50. Pair of candlesticks, each formed as a girl holding a fish. H: ~9". Price B.

Figure 199.51. Scotsman. H: 9". This base form is only otherwise recorded on figures emblematic of the seasons (figs. 155.53–55). Price B.

200. Busts

Figure 200.1. *SHAKESPEAR*. Bust of William Shakespeare. Attributed to Ralph Wood; impressed "112". H: 9.6". William Shakespeare (1564–1616) is England's best-known poet. After the head on the figure of Shakespeare in Westminster Abbey, designed by William Kent and executed by Peter Scheemakers. Price B. *Wisbech & Fenland Museum*.

Figure 200.2. Bust of William Shakespeare. H: ~10". Price B. *Andrew Dando Antiques*.

Figure 200.3. Bust of William Shakespeare. H: 9.3". Price B. *Andrew Dando Antiques*.

Figure 200.4. *W SHAKESPEAR*. Bust of William Shakespeare. H: 17". Price B. *Andrew Dando Antiques*.

Figure 200.5. Bust of William Shakespeare. H: 9". Price B. Northeast Auctions.

Figure 200.6. Bust of William Shakespeare. Impressed "Bott & Co". H: 16". Price B. © *Victoria and Albert Museum, London*.

Figure 200.7. Bust of John Milton. H: 11.5". Impressed "MILTON" behind. John Milton (1608–1674) was an English poet. After the marble bust by John Michael Rysbrack installed in Westminster Abbey in 1737. Price B. *Andrew Dando Antiques.*

Figure 200.8. Bust of John Milton. H: ~11.5". Impressed "MILTON" behind. Beneath the pedestal, "90" is painted and a quartered circle is impressed. Price B. © *Victoria and Albert Museum, London.*

Figure 200.9. *Milton* (incised on front edge of socle). Bust of John Milton. H: 10.5". Price B. *John Howard; www.antiquepottery.co.uk.*

Figure 200.10. Bust of John Milton. Attributed to Ralph Wood; impressed "128". H: 6.9". Frank Falkner notes a small Ralph Wood bust of Milton impressed "127" that is probably like this bust. Falkner states it differs from the larger Ralph Wood bust of Milton that he records as impressed "81". Price A. *Robert Hawker.*

Figure 200.11. Bust of John Milton. H: 9.8". The busts in figures 200.86 and 200.145 are on socles of the same form. Price A. *Martyn Edgell Antiques Ltd.*

Figure 200.12. Bust of Laurence Sterne. H: 9". Laurence Sterne (1713–1768), the Anglo-Irish novelist, is best remembered for *Tristram Shandy*. The bust is after a marble bust by Joseph Nollekens, 1766. Price B. *Martyn Edgell Antiques Ltd.*

Figure 200.13. Bust of Alexander Pope. H: 9.5". Alexander Pope (1688–1744) was an English poet. The bust is after a sculpture by Louis-Francois Roubiliac, completed in 1738. Price B. *Andrew Dando Antiques.*

Figure 200.14. Bust of James Thomson. H: 6.5". The Scottish poet James Thomson (1700–1748) is best known for "The Seasons". Price B. © *Victoria and Albert Museum, London.*

Figure 200.15. Pair of busts of Matthew Prior (L) and James Thomson (R). H: 6.5". Price B. *Nick Burton.*

Figure 200.16. Bust of Matthew Prior. H: 9". Twice impressed "PRIOR" behind. Matthew Prior (1664–1721) was a poet and diplomat. After the bust by Antoine Coysevox that King Louise XIV presented to Prior in 1714, now on Prior's monument in Westminster Abbey. Price B. *Wisbech & Fenland Museum.*

Figure 200.17. Reverse of the previous bust of Matthew Prior. *Wisbech & Fenland Museum.*

Figure 200.18. Bust of Matthew Prior. H: 9.6". Busts of this form were first made in porcelain. Price B. *Collection of Arnold and Barbara Berlin.*

Figure 200.19. Bust of Joseph Addison. H: 8". Painted "Addison" behind. Joseph Addison (1672–1719) was an English poet, playwright, and essayist. Price B. *Elinor Penna*.

Figure 200.20. Bust of Joseph Addison. H: 7.8". Price B. *Woolley and Wallis Salisbury Salerooms Ltd*.

Figure 200.21. Bust of John Locke. H: 8.3". John Locke (1632–1704) was a very influential English philosopher and Enlightenment thinker. Price B. *Image courtesy of The Potteries Museum & Art Gallery, Stoke-on-Trent, UK*.

Figure 200.22. Bust of John Locke. H: 8". Price A. *Stair Galleries*.

Figure 200.23. Bust of Sir Isaac Newton. H: 9.5". Impressed "NEWTON" behind. Sir Isaac Newton (1642–1727) was an influential scientist. After a plaster attributed to John Cheer or Hoskins and Grant and now in the Victoria and Albert Museum (A10-1977). Price B. *Andrew Dando Antiques*.

Figure 200.24. Bust of Sir Isaac Newton. H: 8.9". Impressed "NEWTON" behind. Price B. © *Victoria and Albert Museum, London*.

Figure 200.25. Bust of Handel. Impressed "Ra Wood" and "80". "H: 8.9". The composer George Frideric Handel (1685–1759) became a naturalized British citizen in 1727. Probably after a work by Louis-Francois Roubiliac. Resembles a relief plaque of Handel by Roubiliac, circa 1750–1760 (Victoria and Albert Museum A.11-1961). Price A. *Image courtesy of The Potteries Museum & Art Gallery, Stoke-on-Trent, UK.*

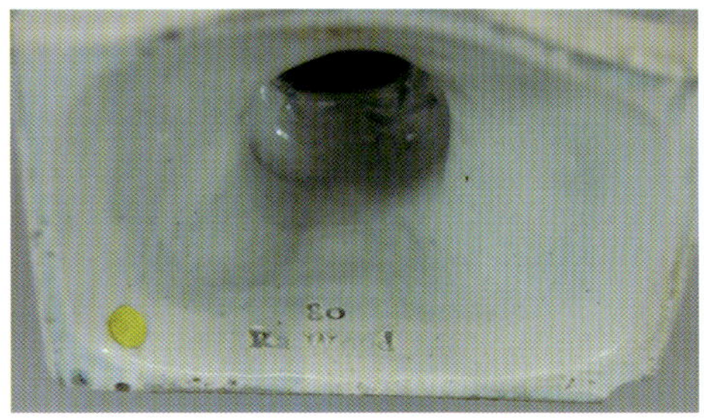

Figure 200.26. The interior of the socle of the previous bust of Handel. The mark "Ra. Wood Burslem" is frequently impressed on busts without "Burslem," suggesting that limited space did not accommodate the full stamp. *Image courtesy of The Potteries Museum & Art Gallery, Stoke-on-Trent, UK.*

Figure 200.27. Bust of Handel. H: 8.7". Price B. *© Victoria and Albert Museum, London.*

Figure 200.28. *VOLTAIRE*. Bust of Voltaire (François-Marie Arouet). Probably made by Ralph Wood. H: 8.3". Titled in typical Ralph Wood script. Voltaire (1694–1778) was a French Enlightenment writer and philosopher. After the painting by Nicolas de Largillière, 1718. Price B. *Woolley and Wallis Salisbury Salerooms Ltd.*

Figure 200.29. Bust of Voltaire. H: 6.5". Impressed "VOLTAIRE" behind. Price A. *Wisbech & Fenland Museum.*

Figure 200.30. Bust of Voltaire, reverse of previous example. "VOLTAIRE" is impressed on the lower edge of the socle. *Wisbech & Fenland Museum.*

Figure 200.31. Bust of Voltaire. H: 6". Price B. *Andrew Dando Antiques.*

Figure 200.32. Bust of Jean-Jacques Rousseau. H: 7". Impressed "ROSSEAU" behind. Rousseau (1712–1778) was a Swiss philosopher, author, and composer. After a portrait by J. H. Taraval. London plaster makers supplied Wedgwood with a bust of Rousseau, and Derby made a similar bust, circa 1780. Price B. *Nick Burton.*

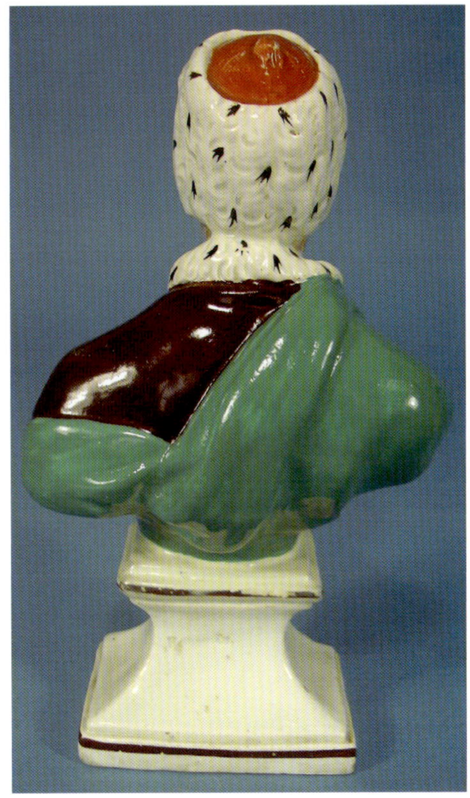

Figure 200.33. Bust of Rousseau, reverse of previous example. "ROUSSEAU" is impressed on the socle. *Nick Burton.*

Figure 200.34. *ROUSSEAU* (impressed on front of socle). Bust of Jean-Jacques Rousseau. H: 7". Price B. © *Victoria and Albert Museum, London.*

Figure 200.35. Bust of Seneca. H: ~5". Seneca (circa 4 B.C.E.–65 C.E.) was a Roman philosopher and statesman. A similarly sized companion bust of Homer is recorded. Price A. *Andrew Dando Antiques.*

Figure 200.36. Bust of Cicero. H: 5.3". Impressed "CICERO" behind. Cicero (106–43 B.C.E.) was a Roman orator, philosopher, and lawyer. Price A. *Image courtesy of The Potteries Museum & Art Gallery, Stoke-on-Trent, UK.*

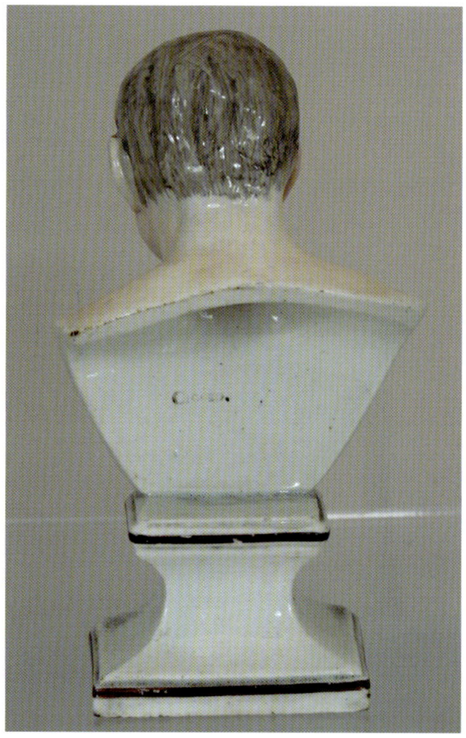

Figure 200.37. Bust of Cicero, reverse of previous example. "CICERO" is impressed on the bust.

Figure 200.38. Bust of Demosthenes. H: 5.5". Impressed "DEMOSTHENES" behind. Demosthenes (384–322 B.C.E.) was a famous Greek orator. Companion to the previous bust of Cicero, and the title is similarly impressed on the reverse. Price A. *Image courtesy of The Potteries Museum & Art Gallery, Stoke-on-Trent, UK.*

Figure 200.39. Bust of Demosthenes. H: 5.3". Price A. *Wisbech & Fenland Museum.*

Figure 200.40. Busts of Plato (L) and Homer (R). Both impressed "E. WOOD". H: 15" (L), 13.5" (R). Plato and Homer were notable ancient Greeks. Plato was a philosopher and mathematician, and Homer was an epic poet. Like the following busts but marked differently. Price C. *Aurea Carter Antiques.*

Figure 200.41. Bust of Homer. Impressed "ENOCH WOOD". H: 12.3". Like the previous bust of Homer but with a different Enoch Wood mark. Companion to the following bust, similarly marked. These busts were reproduced circa 1900 but these are thought to be early. Price B. *Wisbech & Fenland Museum.*

Figure 200.42. Bust of Plato. Impressed "ENOCH WOOD". H: 13". Companion to the previous bust of Homer. Price B. *Wisbech & Fenland Museum.*

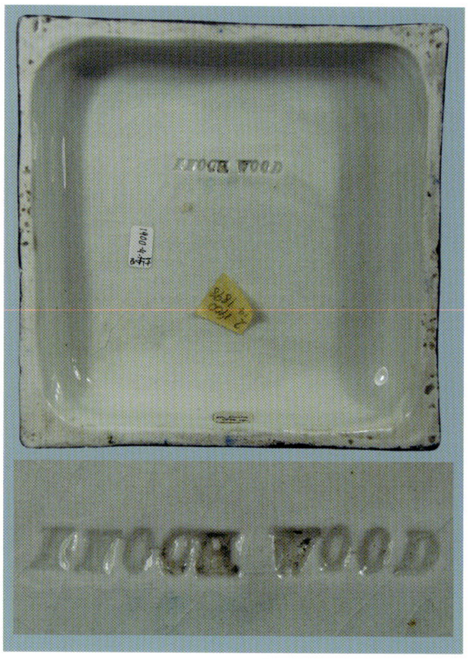

Figure 200.43. Base of the previous bust of Plato showing the "ENOCH WOOD" mark. The companion bust of Homer is similarly marked. *Wisbech & Fenland Museum*

Figure 200.44. Bust of Plato. H: ~14". Price B.

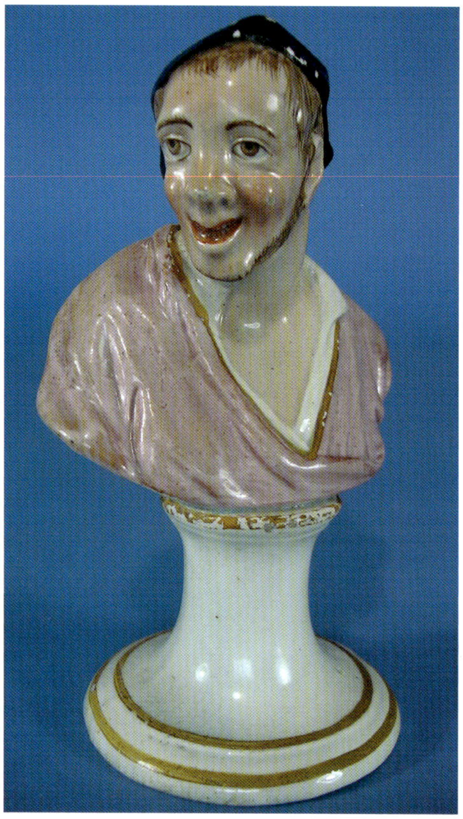

Figure 200.45. Bust of Democritus. H: 5.5". Democritus (circa 460–370 B.C.E.), a Greek philosopher and founder of atomic theory, is known as the "laughing philosopher" because he found man's condition ridiculous. After a Derby bust, circa 1780, derived from Johann Christoff Ludwig Lücke's model, circa 1757. Companion to following bust. Price A. *Nick Burton.*

Figure 200.46. Bust of Heraclitus. H: 5.5". Heraclitus (circa 540–475 B.C.E.) is known as the "weeping philosopher" because he found man's condition melancholy. Companion to previous bust and also after a Derby bust, circa 1780. Price A. *Nick Burton.*

Figure 200.47. Bust, possibly Napoleon. H: 8.8". Napoleon Bonaparte (1769–1821) was a military and political leader in the French Revolution. Under his leadership, French forces threw Europe into turmoil, and he was finally defeated at the Battle of Waterloo in 1815. Price B. © *Victoria and Albert Museum, London.*

Figure 200.48. Bust of Napoleon. H: 9.8". This bust is also recorded impressed "BONAPARTE" on the reverse. Price C. *Andrew Dando Antiques.*

Figure 200.49. Bust of Napoleon. Marked "W.H.J". H: 9.4". The body is feldspathic ironstone. Price B. © *Victoria and Albert Museum, London.*

Figure 200.50. Bust of Napoleon. H: 10.2". Price B. *Andrew Dando Antiques.*

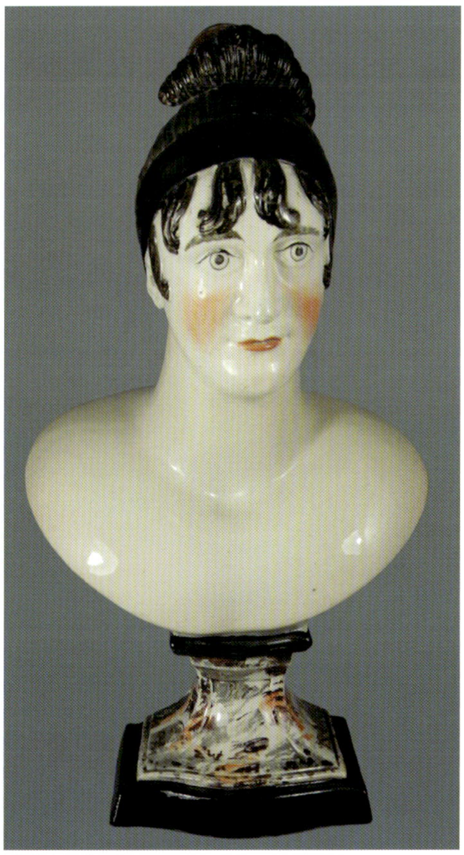

Figure 200.51. Bust of the Empress Josephine. H: 12". Josephine de Beauharnais, Napoleon Bonaparte's first wife, was the first Empress of France. Price C. *The William Herbert and Nancy Hunt Collection.*

Figure 200.52. Bust of the Empress Josephine, reverse of the previous bust. A similar bust is inscribed "Thomas Gruitt 1809" on the reverse. *The William Herbert and Nancy Hunt Collection.*

Figure 200.53. Bust of Czar Alexander I of Russia. Impressed "WOOD & CALDWELL". H: 11.5". Alexander (b. 1777) ruled as Emperor of Russia from 1801 to 1825. The bust strongly resembles earlier portraits of Alexander, which probably assisted in its modeling. Price B. *Andrew Dando Antiques.*

Figure 200.54. Reverse of previous bust impressed "ALEXANDER AEt 35 MOSCOW BURNT EUROPE PRESERVED. 1812" and "WOOD & CALDWELL BURSLEM, Staffordshire". *Andrew Dando Antiques.*

Figure 200.55. Bust of Czar Alexander I of Russia. Impressed "WOOD & CALDWELL". H: 11.4". The medallion on the back is as on the previous bust. This bust also occurs in a 27" size.[1] Price B. © *Victoria and Albert Museum, London.*

Figure 200.56. Bust of George Washington. Impressed "Ra. Wood Burslem". H: 9.7". "WASHINGTON" impressed behind. George Washington (1732–1799) was the first president of the United States of America. Price D. *The William Herbert and Nancy Hunt Collection.*

Figure 200.57. Bust of George Washington. H: 8.8". Price C. *John Howard; www.antiquepottery.co.uk.*

Figure 200.58. Bust of George Washington. Made by Enoch Wood. H: 8.4". Price C. *Elinor Penna.*

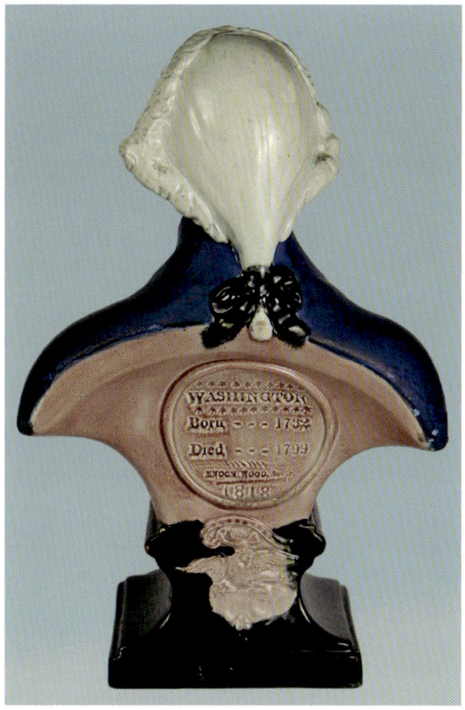

Figure 200.59. Bust of George Washington, reverse of previous example. *Elinor Penna.*

Figure 200.60. Medallion on the reverse of the previous bust of George Washington. It reads, "WASHINGTON Born 1732 Died 1799. ENOCH WOOD, Sculp 1818". *Elinor Penna.*

Figure 200.61. *WELLINGTON* (impressed on lower edge of socle). Bust of the Duke of Wellington. Impressed "WOOD & CALDWELL". H: 11.5". Arthur Wellesley, 1st Duke of Wellington (1769–1852) defeated Napoleon at the Battle of Waterloo in 1815. After Joseph Nolleken's marble bust, 1813. Price B. *Wisbech & Fenland Museum.*

Figure 200.62. Reverse of previous bust of Wellington. The "WOOD & CALDWELL" mark is on the lower edge of the socle. A similar 22" bust (marked) is in The Potteries Museum. *Wisbech & Fenland Museum.*

Figure 200.63. Bust of the Duke of York. H: 5.7". "DUKE OF YORK" impressed behind. Prince Frederick, Duke of York (1763–1827) was the second son of King George III. He commanded the British Army during the French Revolutionary and Napoleonic wars. Price A. *Andrew Dando Antiques.*

Figure 200.64. Bust of the Duke of York. H: 5.7". The bust strongly resembles contemporary likenesses of the Duke, but its design source is unknown. Price A. *Martyn Edgell Antiques Ltd.*

Figure 200.65. Bust of the Duke of York. H: 6". Impressed "DUKE OF YORK" behind. Price A. *Andrew Dando Antiques.*

Figure 200.66. Bust of Horatio Nelson. H: 6.1". "NELSON" impressed behind. 1st Viscount Nelson (1758–1805) was an inspirational naval leader who is best remembered for his victory at Trafalgar, during which he was killed. Price A. *Andrew Dando Antiques.*

Figure 200.67. Bust of Horatio Nelson, reverse of previous bust. *Andrew Dando Antiques.*

Figure 200.68. Bust of Horatio Nelson. H: ~6.1". Price A.

Figure 200.69. Bust of Byron. H ~6". George Gordon Byron (1788–1824) was an important British poet. His lifestyle made him an international celebrity. Price A.

Figure 200.70. Bust of Byron. Attributed to "Sherratt". H: 5.8". "Byron" incised behind. The painting of the socle is typical of "Sherratt". The coat of arms is also on pearlware boxes attributed to "Sherratt". Busts of Nelson and the Duke of York are recorded on the same socle.[2] Price A.

Figure 200.71. Bust of Byron, detail of previous example. This motif of a coat of arms incorporating the Prince of Wales's feathers beneath a crown only appears on "Sherratt" examples (Vol. 3, fig. 120.85, and fig. 198.8). Here the initials "GR" possibly mark the 1820 coronation of King George IV.

Figure 200.72. *S.F.B.* Bust of Sir Frances Burdett. H: 16.5". Sir Frances Burdett (1770–1844) was a popular radical reformer. Price B. *Woolley and Wallis Salisbury Salerooms Ltd.*

Figure 200.73. *H HUNT ESQ.* H: 9.5". Henry "Orator" Hunt (1773–1835) was a well-born British radical agitator who campaigned for parliamentary reform and improved working conditions. Price B. *The William Herbert and Nancy Hunt Collection.*

Figure 200.74. Bust of Lord Canning. H: 5.3". "LORD CANNING" impressed behind. The British statesman George Canning (1770–1827) served as prime minister in 1827. Price A. *Bonhams.*

Figure 200.75. Bust of King George III. Probably made by Enoch Wood/Wood & Caldwell. H: 12.1". King George III (b. 1738) ruled Britain from 1760 to 1820. Price D. © *Victoria and Albert Museum, London.*

Figure 200.76. Bust of King William IV. H: 19.5". King William (b. 1765) ruled Britain from 1830 to 1837. Price C. *Image courtesy of The Potteries Museum & Art Gallery, Stoke-on-Trent, UK.*

Figure 200.77. Bust of King William IV. Attributed to "Sherratt". H: ~11". Price C.

Figure 200.78. *KING WILLIAM THE IV.* Bust of King William IV. Attributed to "Sherratt". H: ~10". Price C.

Figure 200.79. *QUEEN ADDERLENE.* Queen Adelaide. Attributed to "Sherratt". H: 10". Queen Adelaide (1792–1849) was the devoted consort of King William IV. Price C. *The William Herbert and Nancy Hunt Collection.*

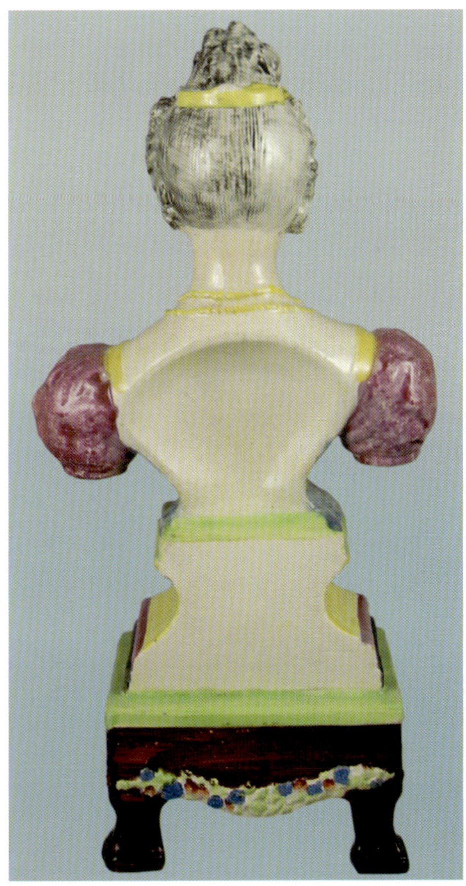

Figure 200.80. Bust of Queen Adelaide, reverse of previous example. *The William Herbert and Nancy Hunt Collection.*

Figure 200.81. *Addaide*. Bust of Queen Adelaide. H: 8.5". Porcelainous body. Price C. *John Howard; www.antiquepottery.co.uk.*

Figure 200.82. Figure 200.1. Bust of Jan Willem de Winter. H: 8". De Winter (1761–1812) was a Dutch Admiral. He was captured when he battled the British fleet under Admiral Duncan at Camperdown.[3] Price B. *Andrew Dando Antiques.*

Figure 200.83. Bust of Rear Admiral Sir Edward Berry. H: 10.5". Incised behind "Captain Berry" and "Thomas Greatbatch 1809". Sir Edward Berry (1768–1831) rose to Rear Admiral in the Royal Navy. Price B. *Clars Auction Galleries.*

Figure 200.84. Bust of a military officer, probably Rear Admiral Sir Edward Berry. H: 8.5". Berry is best remembered for his role as flag captain on Nelson's ship at the Battle of the Nile. Price B. *Andrew Dando Antiques.*

Figure 200.85. Bust of a military officer, possibly Nelson. H: 8.5". Price B. *Andrew Dando Antiques.*

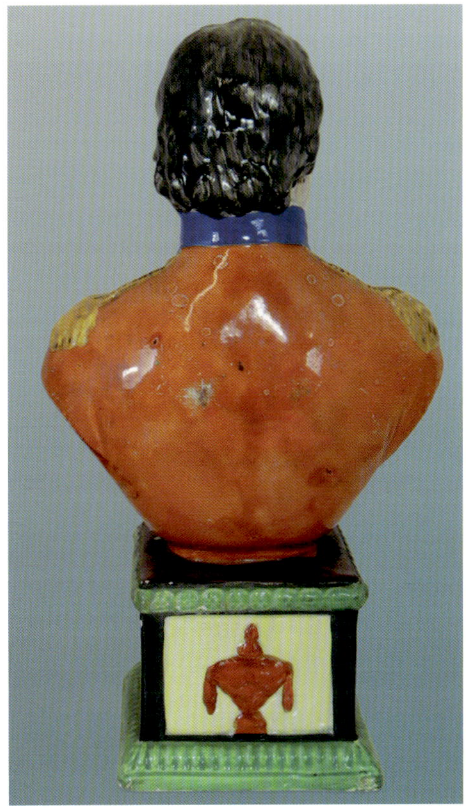

Figure 200.86. Bust of a military officer, possibly Nelson. H: 9.4". The busts in figures 200.11 and 200.145 are on socles of the same form. Price B. *Image courtesy of The Potteries Museum & Art Gallery, Stoke-on-Trent, UK.*

Figure 200.87. Bust of a military officer, reverse of previous bust. *Image courtesy of The Potteries Museum & Art Gallery, Stoke-on-Trent, UK.*

Figure 200.88. Bust of a military officer. H: 8". Companion to the following bust. Impressed beneath "J JARVIS JANUARY 12 TH 1836". Price B. *John Howard; www.antiquepottery.co.uk.*

Figure 200.89. Bust of a military officer, probably Nelson. H: 8". Companion to the previous bust. Impressed beneath "J JARVIS JANUARY 12 TH 1836". A similar bust marked "NELSON" and "Stephan P", probably the mark of the modeler Pierre Stephan, is in the National Maritime Museum, Greenwich (AAA6023). Price B. *John Howard; www.antiquepottery.co.uk.*

Figure 200.90. Busts of military officers, the previous two busts, showing the impression beneath. Both busts are marked in the same way. *John Howard; www.antiquepottery.co.uk.*

Figure 200.91. Bust of a military officer, possibly Sir John Moore. H: 10.8". Sir John Moore (1761–1809) is known for his leadership in the Peninsula War. Price B. *Wisbech & Fenland Museum.*

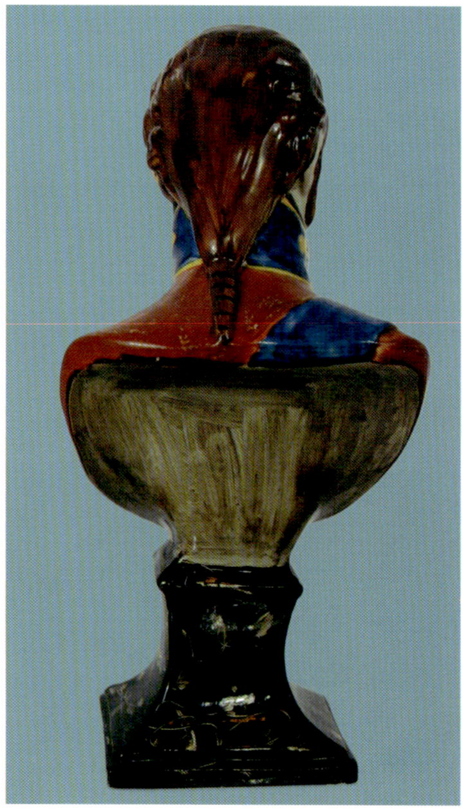

Figure 200.92. Bust of a military officer, reverse of the previous bust. *Wisbech & Fenland Museum.*

Figure 200.93. Bust of a military officer, possibly Sir John Moore. H: 10.3". Price B. *The William Herbert and Nancy Hunt Collection.*

Figure 200.94. Bust of a military officer. H: 8". Price B. *Image courtesy of The Potteries Museum & Art Gallery, Stoke-on-Trent, UK.*

Figure 200.95. Bust of a military officer, reverse of previous bust. *Image courtesy of The Potteries Museum & Art Gallery, Stoke-on-Trent, UK.*

Figure 200.96. Bust of a military officer, possibly Admiral Lord Duncan. H: 7.6". Admiral Adam Duncan, 1st Viscount Duncan (1731–1804) defeated the Dutch in a decisive battle near Camperdown in 1797. Price B. *Andrew Dando Antiques.*

Figure 200.97. Bust of a gentleman, possibly William Pitt the Younger. H: 8.6". William Pitt the Younger (1759–1806) became prime minister at the age of 24 and held that office through the wars with France and Napoleon. Price C. *Andrew Dando Antiques.*

Figure 200.98. Bust of Admiral John Jervis, later the Earl St. Vincent. Impressed "HERCULANEUM" beneath. H: 8.9". Made at the Herculaneum Pottery, Liverpool. Jervis is remembered for defeating the Spanish fleet at the Battle of Cape Saint Vincent in 1797. Pierre Stephan may have modeled the bust, perhaps after Francis Cotes's portrait of Jervis. Price C. *John Howard; www.antiquepottery.co.uk.*

Figure 200.99. *MISS FOOT*. Bust of Maria Foote. Attributed to "Sherratt". H: 11.5". Maria Foote (circa 1797–1867) was an actress and renowned beauty. Price B.

Figure 200.100. Bust of Maria Foote. Attributed to "Sherratt". H: 11.5". Price B. *Collection of Arnold and Barbara Berlin.*

Figure 200.101. Bust of Maria Foote. Attributed to "Sherratt". H: 12". Price B. *Image courtesy of The Potteries Museum & Art Gallery, Stoke-on-Trent, UK.*

Figure 200.102. Bust of Maria Foote as Venus. H: 7.7" "Venus" is painted behind. On December 26, 1832, Miss Foote debuted as Venus in Paphian Bower, or Venus and Adonis. Price A. *Martyn Edgell Antiques Ltd.*

Figure 200.103. Bust of an actor. H: 7.7". Possibly the popular comedian Charles Matthews (1776–1835) or the actor T. P. Cooke (Thomas Potter Cooke, 1786–1864). Price B. *Martyn Edgell Antiques Ltd.*

Figure 200.104. Bust of an actor. H: 8". Like the previous bust. Here, the socle is modeled after a ship's capstan, and this lends credibility to the bust portraying T. P. Cooke who personified the British sailor on the stage. Price B. *Martyn Edgell Antiques Ltd.*

Figure 200.105. Bust of Minerva, goddess of wisdom. Impressed "MINERVA" behind. H: 12.2". Price C. *Andrew Dando Antiques.*

Figure 200.106. Bust of Minerva. H 12.5". Price C. *Andrew Dando Antiques.*

Figure 200.107. Bust of Minerva. H: 12.5". The use of silver luster on the helmet indicates this bust was not made before 1805, the year in which silver lustering was introduced commercially. Price C.

Figure 200.108. Bust emblematic of air. Impressed "LEEDS POTTERY". H: 6.5". His puffed cheeks suggest blowing, and his cloak is of eagle skin. Price B. © *Victoria and Albert Museum, London*

Figure 200.109. Bust emblematic of water. Attributed to Leeds Pottery. H: 6.5". A dolphin's head is molded beneath her garment. Price B. © *Victoria and Albert Museum, London.*

Figure 200.110. Pair of busts, emblematic of fire (L) and earth (R). Attributed to Leeds Pottery. H: 7". Fire has flames atop his head. Earth wears a lion skin and is portrayed as Cybele, the Earth Mother, whose attributes include lions. Price B. *Aurea Carter Antiques.*

Figure 200.111. Bust of Cybele, the Earth Mother. H: 6.2". Price A. *The William Herbert and Nancy Hunt Collection.*

Figure 200.112. Bust of Neptune, the Roman god of the sea. Impressed "NEPTUNE" and "R Wood B" (for "Ra. Wood Burslem") behind. H: 11.8". Price C. *Wisbech & Fenland Museum.*

Figure 200.113. Reverse of the socle of the previous bust of Neptune. The impressed title and partially impressed Ralph Wood mark are visible. *Wisbech & Fenland Museum.*

Figure 200.114. *NEPTUNE*. Bust of Neptune. Attributed to Ralph Wood. H: 11.8". Price C. *Andrew Dando Antiques.*

Figure 200.115. Bust of Neptune, H: ~14". Because Neptune is the Roman god of the sea, he is draped with a fish-like garment. Price B.

Figure 200.116. Bust of Neptune. H: 13.6". "1826" is inscribed on the reverse. Price B. *Martyn Edgell Antiques Ltd.*

Figure 200.117. Busts of Neptune (L) and Hercules (R), a pair. H: 14". On the reverse, Neptune is inscribed "G.R" and impressed "1811", and Hercules is inscribed "1811". Neptune is from different molds than previous examples. Hercules wears the skin of the ferocious Nemean lion that he strangled. Price D. *John Howard; www.antiquepottery.co.uk.*

Figure 200.118. Reverse of previous bust of Neptune, impressed "1811" and inscribed "G.R". *John Howard; www.antiquepottery.co.uk.*

Figure 200.119. Bust of the Madonna (Mater Dolorosa). H: 15". Price B. *Andrew Dando Antiques.*

Figure 200.120. Bust of the Madonna (Mater Dolorosa). H: 16.6". Price B. © *Victoria and Albert Museum, London.*

Figure 200.121. Bust of the Madonna (Mater Dolorosa). Impressed "SADNESS" and "WEDGWOOD". H: 22.2". Note the large size. Price C. © *Victoria and Albert Museum, London.*

Figure 200.122. Bust of Zingara. Impressed "EGYPTIAN PRIESTESS" and "Ra. Wood Burslem". H: 11". In 1747, Peter Scheemakers sold plaster busts of "Zingara Egyptian Woman" after a Greek marble from the Villa Borghese (listed as "An Egyptian Woman"), now at Versailles. Circa 1775, Wedgwood and Derby made busts like this in basalt and porcelain respectively, after plaster models. Price C.

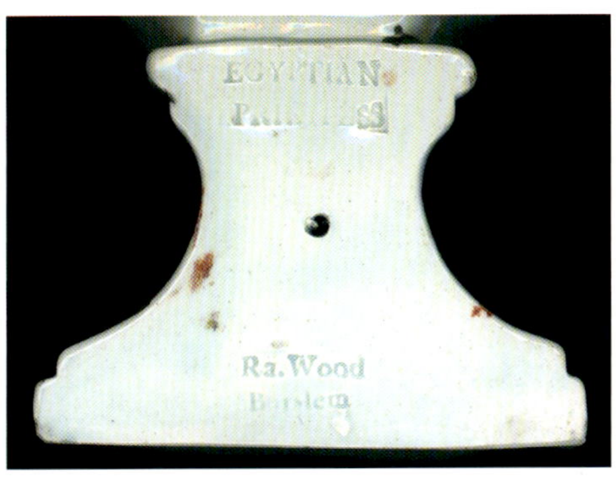

Figure 200.123. Reverse of the socle of the previous bust of Zingara. The impressed title "EGYPTIAN PRIESTESS" and "Ra. Wood Burslem" are visible. Ralph Wood busts are sometimes instead marked on the interior of the socle.

Figure 200.124. Bust of Zingara, impressed "ZINGARA" behind. Attributed to Ralph Wood and impressed "92". H: 10.5". Zingara (meaning "gypsy" in Italian) was the gypsy heroine of a burletta, *La Zingara: Or, The Gipsy,* first produced in April 1773. Price B. © *Victoria and Albert Museum, London.*

Figure 200.125. Bust of Zingara. H: ~10.5". Apparently from the same molds as the previous Ralph Wood examples but with no discernible Ralph Wood characteristics and possibly made by another potter. Price B.

Figure 200.126. Bust of Zingara. H: 10.7". Price B. *© Victoria and Albert Museum, London.*

Figure 200.127. Bust of a classical lady. H: 19.5". It has been suggested that this bust portrays the youthful Princess Charlotte (fig. 200.147), but that seems unlikely. Price B. *Image courtesy of The Potteries Museum & Art Gallery, Stoke-on-Trent, UK.*

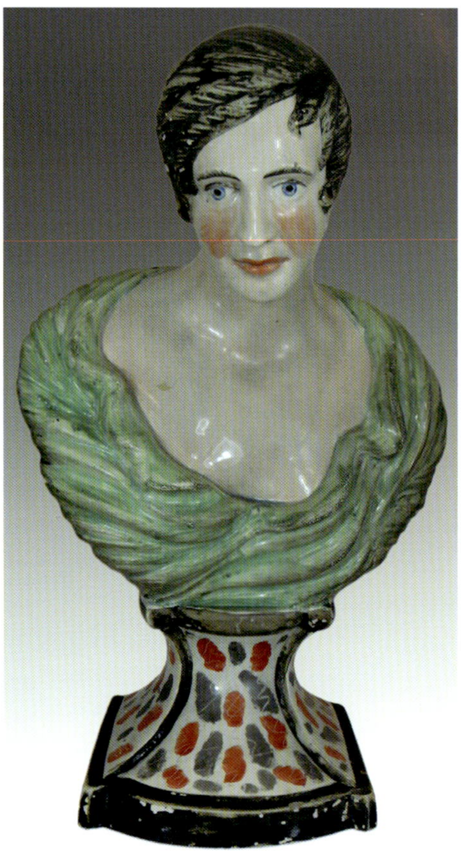

Figure 200.128. Bust of a classical lady. H: 13.5". Price B. *Image courtesy of The Potteries Museum & Art Gallery, Stoke-on-Trent, UK.*

Figure 200.129. *REV JOHN WESLEY.* Bust of the Rev. John Wesley. Attributed to "Sherratt". H: ~12". John Wesley (1703–1791), a Church of England cleric and theologian, founded the Methodist movement. Price C.

Figure 200.130. Bust of the Rev. John Wesley. Attributed to "Sherratt". H: ~12". Wesley and his teachings were enormously influential in the Potteries, and busts of Wesley abound. Price C. *John Howard; www.antiquepottery.co.uk.*

Figure 200.131. Bust of the Rev. John Wesley. H: 12". Price B. *John Howard; www.antiquepottery.co.uk.*

Figure 200.132. Bust of the Rev. John Wesley. H: 11.7". Price B. *John Howard; www.antiquepottery.co.uk.*

Figure 200.133. Bust of the Rev. John Wesley. H: 11.5". Price B. *Martyn Edgell Antiques Ltd.*

Figure 200.134. Bust of the Rev. John Wesley. H: 4.6". Note the petite size. Price. A. *Brighton and Hove Museums.*

Figure 200.135. Bust of the Rev. John Wesley. Made by Enoch Wood. H: 11". Impressed behind "THE REVD. JOHN WESLEY MA AGED 88". This is an early edition of Enoch Wood's famous bust of Wesley, made in 1781. Wood refined the drapery for subsequent editions. Price B. *Wisbech & Fenland Museum.*

Figure 200.136. Reverse of the previous bust of John Wesley. This form of medallion and inscription are found on the earliest Wood busts of Wesley, but Wesley's age is usually stated as 81. *Wisbech & Fenland Museum.*

The figures of a boy with his dog and a girl with a lamb (figs. 201.3, 201.4) are also reproductions. The shade of green on their bases and the awkward bocages betray their lack of age. On the reverse, both figures have clearly visible holes to enable venting during firing. On pre-Victorian figures, a vent hole is never this obvious. When needed, vent holes were placed with great thought, and finding them can be a game of sorts. Both figures are marked on the reverse with "WALTON" impressed within a banner. A maker's mark on a figure implies authenticity, but on these figures the mark is spurious. John Walton was an early nineteenth-century potter who impressed his name in a similar manner, but these figures were not made by John Walton. Firstly, the letters in "WALTON" should be impressed deeply and should have well-defined serifs. Some earlier reproductions almost pull this off, but most have letters that lack serifs. Secondly, John Walton made figures of this form—but he did not make them atop square bases. A mere verbal description of these figures would convey that they are not "the real thing". Another well-known reproduction figure sporting the Walton name is titled *TENDERNESS*. It displays similar tell-tale signs of its newness. While reproductions of this sort may well be approaching antiquity, their value is minimal.

Figure 201.5. Reproduction figure of a sportsman (L) alongside an early example (R). H: 7.3". The reproduction sportsman and his dog are expressionless and frozen. Crude crazing is apparent on the reproduction figure but not on the early figure. Left: *Andrew Dando Antiques' Black Museum.*

The two sportsmen in figure 201.5 were made about a century apart. The figure on the right was made around 1820, but the figure on the left is a much later reproduction. The differences in the modeling and painting are obvious. On the reproduction, the rigid poses and expressionless faces of both the sportsman and his dog, in conjunction with the colors of the mound beneath their feet, betray a more recent origin. Also, the reproduction figure is heavily and obviously crazed. Early figures do exhibit crazing, but it seldom jumps out to greet you. Instead, the pattern is usually fine and one often has to look carefully to detect it.

Figure 201.6. Reproduction (L) and genuine (R) examples of the vicar and Moses. H: 9" each. The modeling and painting of the reproduction figure is clumsy. The colors of the body and glaze and the very obvious crazing betray its recent manufacture. Left: *Andrew Dando Antiques' Black Museum.* Right: *John Howard; www.antiquepottery.co.uk.*

Like the sportsmen, the Vicar and Moses groups in 201.6 differ vastly in age. The group on the left is a reproduction, and an earlier example is alongside it. The early group oozes features that are not present on the newer group. On the early group, both faces are nicely modeled, and the eyebrows and the clerk's eyes are carefully painted with many brush strokes, but on the reproduction that detail is lost. Importantly, the latter figure exhibits the abnormally large crazing found on many reproductions. Handling it will provide additional information. The thick, tactile glazes associated with early figures will not be evident, and the clear glaze and whitish body will be typical of later figures. Examples of a vicar and Moses group incised "R. WOOD 1794" exist. These were manufactured by the 1920s, so now they are almost antique in their own right. But they were not made by Ralph Wood, and they were not made in 1794.

Figure 201.7. Twentieth-century examples of Jobson and Nell. H: 14". Note the heavy crazing, the poor modeling, and the tonality. *Image courtesy of The Potteries Museum & Art Gallery, Stoke-on-Trent, UK.*

Figure 201.8. Comparison of the faces of reproduction (L) and early (R) examples of Jobson and Nell. The early examples have well defined, animated expressions. *Image courtesy of The Potteries Museum & Art Gallery, Stoke-on-Trent, UK.*

In the early 1800s, figures of a cobbler (Jobson) and his wife (Nell) were popular, and this subject enjoyed a revival of sorts a century later. Originally, the figures were made in two sizes. Smaller pairs are around six inches in height, and big pairs are around fourteen inches. From the early 1900s, pairs were made in just these sizes, probably using original molds (fig. 201.7). Again, the later figures are in a color palette that does not occur on early figures and they often exhibit large, very obvious crazing not typical of early figures. Of course, the later figures lack the animation of early examples. Placed side by side, the difference in expressions is astounding (fig. 201.8).

Figure 201.9. Reproduction sheep with bocage. Impressed "LEEDS POTTERY". H: 5.3". This bocage and its flowers are not documented on early figures. *Andrew Dando Antiques' Black Museum.*

Figures made by the Leeds Pottery can be traps for the unwary. From the 1890s to 1957, J. W. & G. W. Senior operated the Leeds Pottery, and this manufactory used many eighteenth-and nineteenth-century Leeds molds. The sheep group in figure 201.9 is an example of such work. To the informed, it is immediately apparent that the bocage and the flowers are of a form not recorded on early figures. Viewed from beneath, another irregularity jumps out: the unusual dimple in the base (fig. 201.10). An early base was formed by pressing the clay by hand. The depression in the base of the sheep suggests that this base may have been slip-cast—a process whereby liquid clay was poured into a mold. Early figures are never slip-cast. They are always press-molded.

Figure 201.11. Twentieth-century bull baiting group. H: 5.5", L: 7". This reduced-scale model of an early nineteenth-century group lacks the vigor, detail, and color of early examples. *Andrew Dando Antiques' Black Museum.*

Auction houses that should know better routinely fall prey to the small bull-baiting group in figure 201.11 and describe it as being made in the nineteenth century. But this bull-baiting group was definitely made in the twentieth century in an attempt to replicate, at a reduced scale, the larger groups traditionally associated with "Sherratt". Anthony Oliver's *Staffordshire Pottery: the Tribal Art of England*, pages 45 and 48, tells of the Kent factory producing small bull baitings as

Figure 201.10. Base of previous figure showing a dimple. *Andrew Dando Antiques' Black Museum.*

late as 1960. Oliver spoke to the man responsible for reducing the group from the "Sherratt" original. He was very proud of his derivative work and kept an example in a cabinet in his living room.

Other reproductions of early figures abound, as do figures made in the style of early figures. Notably, figures of St. Sebastian (sometimes marked ENOCH WOOD or E. WOOD) appear in a typical early twentieth-century palette. An unpainted figure of this form was excavated among other Enoch Wood figures from the Old Town Hall site in Burslem, but this author has been unable to record an enamel-painted figure that confidently dates to that era. Examples of the Blackheath golfers also frequently masquerade as early figures, but again this author has been unable to locate a single early example, and this group was probably only first manufactured in the twentieth century.

Reproduction figures are not confined to those discussed here, so additional pointers to their detection are offered. Remember that early figures were always press-molded. In this process, the clay was pressed by hand into the molds. As a result, the interiors of figures can be bumpy—although the potters skillfully smoothed the lower surfaces of closed bases. Some (but not all) reproduction figures, on the other hand, are slip-cast. Slip-casting is a liquid process, and it results in the interior of a figure being smooth and of an even thickness that reflects the contour of the exterior. If a figure appears to be slip-cast, it is not an early figure. Also, early figures will not have a printed mark beneath, but some later figures were made with printed marks. The presence of a printed mark raises a red flag. A rough or re-glazed patch on a base suggests a seller may have sanded off a printed mark. One other obvious warning signal is the presence of bright gilding. Early figures (aside from the very largest, such as figures of Shakespeare) almost never show much gilding. If gilding was applied, it was always a soft, subtle gold. Usually, this gold has largely rubbed off over the years, leaving mere traces of its presence. A shiny gold line on a figure is a definite indication of a later date of manufacture.

Figure 201.12. *WIDOW, ELIJAH*. Made in Asia from the late twentieth century. H: 10.3". These are very apparent reproductions. Note the child's unusual head and that the book is integral to her form, not modeled separately as in early examples. *Andrew Dando Antiques' Black Museum.*

Figure 201.13. Base of *WIDOW* in previous example. The base is abnormally thick, crazed, and discolored. Attempts to simulate age include rubbed paint and a crack beneath. Flowers and leaves (normally applied individually) appear to be integral to the form. *Andrew Dando Antiques' Black Museum.*

Figure 201.14. Bocages on reproduction figures of Elijah and the Widow are crude, confused emulations. Elijah's neck is stained to simulate age. *Andrew Dando Antiques' Black Museum.*

In more recent decades, reproductions of Asian origin have flooded the market. These hideous objects are such crude, blatant copies that it is difficult to believe that anyone could mistake them for "the real thing". Unfortunately, they are abundant and they are traps for the uninitiated. The figures of Elijah and the Widow in figures 210.12–14 are typical of this genre. Nothing about these figures is right. Every aspect of their appearance and feel betrays their newness. They are thickly potted. The flat bocages (each seemingly molded as one piece), the thick bases, the unusual expressions (sometimes facial features appear rather oriental), the dense paint...the list goes on. Most obvious is the heavy, dark crazing. Early figures are never crazed in this way. Add to it, the figures are stained and have a good coating of dirt, which, like the crazing, has been deliberately added to simulate age. Some of it removes easily, whereas dirt on an early figure typically has wormed itself into crevices between bocage leaves and behind feet and may only yield to professional cleaning or to gentle but determined probing.

Fortunately, nobody has yet made reproductions of early enamel-painted figures that fool experts—and most should not fool novice collectors. Because they are so available, detectable, and undesirable, reproductions tend to be a lot less expensive than their genuine counterparts. Old figures, on the other hand, are made with materials and techniques that have vanished from our world. They simply cannot be replicated. They have soul. For that reason, they are worth the price we must pay for the privilege of enjoying them in our homes.

202. Evaluating a Figure

Assessing a figure is a demanding task. From the first moment, the senses are under assault as touch and sight together convey a huge amount of information. If the figure is a potential purchase, desire enters the equation. But figures can be costly, and a purchase is usually a commitment to long-term ownership. It is much easier to buy a figure than to sell it, so the head must rule the heart. The following steps are suggested as a guide to determining if a figure is "right".

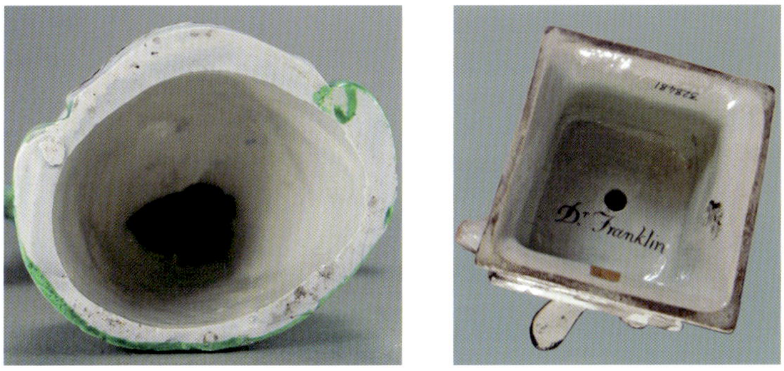

Figure 202.1. Bases of figures, both with well glazed rims. The dirt ingrained in the rim on the right is normal.

Assess the color of the clay and glaze. Turn the figure over. The bottom of a figure may seem an unlikely starting point, but the area beneath the base affords the best opportunity to see the color of the glaze and the body without enamel paint obscuring the view. A blue glaze usually indicates that the figure falls within the pre-Victorian era, but many legitimate figures have clearer glazes, particularly if they were made later in that period. Possibly the interior of the base has been sprayed to conceal restoration. Restoration changes color over time, so any large area of discoloration must be investigated. In figure 202.1, one of the bases reveals an added surprise: the figure's title is painted beneath. There is no end to what a base may reveal. An old price tag or a collector's label is always a pleasing discovery.

Figure 202.2. Figure of Ophelia detached from the base, now lost. The figure stands on a rough, unglazed rim. *Image courtesy of The Potteries Museum & Art Gallery, Stoke-on-Trent, UK.*

Determine if the figure has lost its base. Look at the rim of the base. The very edge of the base, the rim on which the figure stands, should be glazed (fig. 202.1.) The rim may be discolored or have the odd rough spot from centuries of contact with assorted surfaces, but essentially the rim should be glazed. The rim on the right in figure 202.1 is scratched and dirtied, but the glaze is apparent to the eye and to the touch. An unglazed rim can mean one of two things. Perhaps the base was damaged, and a restorer filed down the rim to even it out. This essentially lowers the height of the figure. More likely, an unglazed rim means that the figure has lost what was its true base. Many figures were assembled on a mound-like structure that was then attached to a base (frequently rectangular). The mound and the base melded together in the first firing. Next, the entire figure was dipped in glaze and fired for a second time. The area of contact between the mound and the base escaped getting glazed because the glaze could not reach that area. But if the base was lost at some later date, the edge of the mound was exposed—and it will be unglazed. Figure 202.2 shows a figure of Ophelia. At first glance, she appears complete. However, Ophelia was once mounted on a base. Looking beneath the figure reveals that the rim is rough and unglazed.

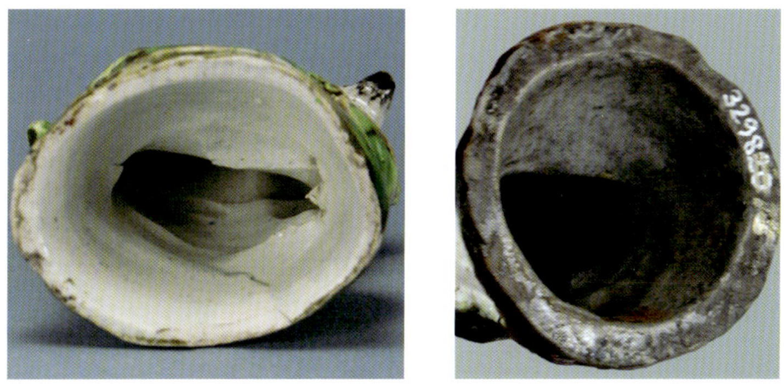

Figure 202.3. Interiors of two figures. Left: a well glazed rim and interior, as should be expected. Right: a base once sealed the entire interior of the figure from glaze. As the base is now lost, an unglazed rim and interior are revealed.

If the figure is open from beneath, look into the figure (fig. 202.3.) Dipping an open figure into glaze is akin to dipping a glass into water: however careful you are, the interior gets wet. A figure that is open and hollow from beneath should show glaze on the rim and well into the figure's interior. But if a base once entirely sealed off the interior of the figure, the interior will not be glazed. And if the base is subsequently lost, the unglazed interior will be revealed. In figure 202.3, it is apparent that both the base rim and interior of the figure on the right escaped being glazed because the presence of a base (now lost) prevented glaze access.

Figure 202.4. *VENUS*. The example on the left has a small figure of Cupid. Cupid is lost from the example on the right, and the spot on which Cupid stood has been crudely dabbed with paint.

Figure 202.5. Shepherd musicians. Despite the different composition of the flocks, both are complete and original. Because figures were manufactured by hand, no two are ever quite identical.

Determine if the figure is complete. Many figures and groups look complete, but you must verify that some part has not been lost. The loss of a major component, such as a bocage or a large figure, is relatively easy to detect, but the devil is in the details. In figure 202.4, Venus on the right looks complete. But compared to Venus on the left, something is missing. The figure on the right has lost the small figure of Cupid that should stand beside Venus. Check photo sources to determine whether the figure you are contemplating is complete. But be aware that figures and groups were made with great variation. The two groups in figure 202.5 are clearly from the same pot bank. The bocages and figures are the same—yet the composition and placement of the animals in the flocks differ. How do you know which is right? In this case, the answer is that both are right. Checking the animals carefully reveals that all are original and all are attached to the bases, as made. Remember, figures were assembled by hand, so there is infinite room for disparity. But if you suspect something is missing from its expected spot, check carefully for a roughness or over-painting. When a component is lost, it usually leaves an irregular patch. On areas that are uneven to begin with, this is sometimes easily concealed. If a small sheep is knocked off the grassy surface of a large, complex group, the scar is easily covered. The loss of a small sheep that nobody will really miss will have relatively little impact on value. But the loss of a small figure of Maria Marten from a Red Barn group or an organ-grinder from a menagerie platform significantly impacts value.

Figure 202.6. Nursery groups. In the group on the right, the boy is of the wrong form. Another early figure has been used to replace the original figure, which was presumably damaged or lost.

Determine if all components are original to each other. If the figure or group is complete, don't be lulled into complacency. If all the components are original, are they original to each other? Nasty things have been done to figures over the past decades in the name of "restoration". Sympathetic restoration done to museum standards is to be applauded, but often that line gets crossed. Look at the nursery groups in figure 202.6. All the components on both groups are original. All the figures on both groups were made in the early 1800s. But comparing the two groups reveals a difference. Look carefully at the boys standing to the right of each base. The boys are different. The boy on the right hand group is a replacement. That group lost the boy, so a restorer took another small figure of a boy, removed the boy from its base and placed it on the empty spot. Comparing this group to photos of several other similar groups reveals that the boy never looks like this. The best intentioned dealer can get caught here. To all intents and purposes, the restoration appears to be nothing more than the reattachment of a part, with no loss of material. Knowledge is power in these matters. Know what your figure should look like. Always scrutinize points of attachment. If there is any indication of reattachment, be certain that the original material was reattached.

Figure 202.7. Britannia. The example on the left is original. The example on the right has an awkward plume and an unnaturally extended arm that invite further investigation.

Know the correct profile of the figure. This is a first step in detecting gross restoration. Extended parts of figures—outstretched hands, plumes on hats, etc.—are easily knocked and broken. Just step back from the figure and look at its shape. Does anything seem awkward or disproportionate? A slightly clunky hand, an awkwardly positioned tail on an animal, or an arm at an unnatural angle can be an early warning sign. In figure 202.7, Britannia on the right appears to have her arm extended at a peculiar angle. This arm must be checked. Comparing the figure to the example on the left and to other images in this work reveals that Britannia's arm is indeed positioned abnormally—almost certainly due to poor restoration. The plume atop the helmet also needs to be checked. This lovely plume is easily damaged. Ignorant restorers will create a plume that resembles a banana, and the cost of redoing the restoration needs to be factored into a purchase decision.

Figure 202.8. *DR SYNTAX STOPPED BY HIGHWAYMEN*. Both examples appear complete, but the example on the right has an entirely restored highwayman, which slashes value. The bocage is also restored.

Figure 202.9. Billy Waters. Left: the larger model that never has a dog. Center: the smaller model typically made with a dog. Right: the smaller model with a dog, as would be expected, but the dog is restored. Center: *Brighton and Hove Museums*.

Assess the extent of restoration. Most figures have had some restoration or repair. This may have minimal impact on value, but gross restoration can destroy a figure's value. Use strong reading glasses and good light to scrutinize your potential purchase. Any restoration inevitably has to be painted, so check the surface carefully for enamel restoration. Restored enamels feel slightly plastic-like to the touch, and if you move a pin across a restored area, it will drag rather than glide. Think of it this way: original glaze is like glass, so a pin flies across it, but restorers' paint is like nail polish, so a pin drags. Does a suspect area look different from the surrounding areas—perhaps there is a subtle shift in color or shine or the fine crazing apparent in adjacent areas is lacking? Look along the arms of figures to see if there is slight change in the way light is reflected. This may be a clue to breakage and subsequent reattachment. This is perhaps the best type of repair to encounter because all original material is present. Look around the bases/feet of small components. If this tells you that a table, for example, has been reattached to the base, look further. Is the table original? What about the items on it? Know that it is possible to restore anything. Heads on figures, even entire figures have been restored, and this affects value significantly. In figure 202.8, both groups portray Doctor Syntax being robbed by a highwayman, but they are not equal. The example on the right has an entirely made-up highwaymen; the example on the left is original. In figure 202.9, Billy Waters on the right has an entirely restored dog. The example in the center has an original dog. Interestingly, the example on the left is larger, and larger examples are consistently made without a dog. Checking for restoration is detective work, and each clue leads you further along the path to knowing what you are buying.

Enamel restoration is one of the most common types of restoration you will encounter. Enamels sometimes flake, and their appearance is then enhanced by applying fresh paint. Minimal restoration of enamels is quite acceptable, but less is definitely more in this case. Gross over-painting of a figure is, simply put, just gross. A figure that has a coating of clear, glossy "stuff" applied to "revitalize" tired enamels will look and feel nasty and should be avoided. Restorers frequently use a spray gun to apply a fine coating of paint. The spray inevitably covers an area larger than the damage it conceals, sometimes making things look worse than they really are. Spraying a small hairline makes a largish area suspect. It really is difficult to know just what happened under the new paint without actually stripping it off. Professional restorers provide reports with their work, and if the seller has used a professional restorer, full details of any restoration will be available.

Figure 202.10. *REMUS & ROMULUS*. The example on the right has an entirely restored bocage and restoration to both children. It is difficult, if not impossible, to restore a bocage to fool the experienced naked eye.

Assess the bocage for restoration or repair. Most bocages have undergone some restoration. Run your fingers along the edge of the bocage. It should feel a little rough. If it feels slick and smooth, it is probably restored. Look in the crevices between the bocage leaves. Dirt is good. It generally means that nobody has paid any attention to the bocage for a long, long time. Be tolerant of damage. There is always a premium for perfection, but minor damage is preferable to restoration. A little damage or restoration to a bocage will not impact value significantly. A totally restored bocage is not a pretty sight, and it drastically reduces value (fig. 202.10).

Figure 202.11. *ST. PAUL*. Although marked "WALTON", this figure has a bocage of a form only found on "Sherratt" figures. Scrutiny reveals that a bocage from another figure has been attached to St. Paul.

Figure 202.13. Charlotte at the tomb of Werther. This figure is on a typical Enoch Wood base, but its Tunstall Group bocage is from some other figure.

Assess the bocage to determine if it is original to the figure. Experienced dealers have been misled by "transplanted" bocages. This happens when a figure loses its bocage, and the deficit is remedied by attaching a bocage from another figure. If well done—and it can be—close scrutiny reveals only that the bocage has been "repaired," the term used to describe the reattachment of original material. To avoid this problem, understand what bocage form you might expect to see with a figure. Thus, "Sherratt"-type bocages never occur on Walton figures—and this combination should raise a red flag. Figure 202.11 shows just that: a figure of St. Paul marked "WALTON" but sporting a combination of bocage leaves and flowers specific to "Sherratt" figures. Scrutiny reveals that the bocage has been attached subsequent to manufacture—and a bocage from a "Sherratt" figure was substituted for the original bocage. Similarly, the charming gardening group in figure 202.12 has a lovely pinecone bocage, of the sort specific to the Patriotic Group, and, to all intents and purposes, the bocage appears to have been repaired. The problem is that the Patriotic Group did not make examples of this gardening group. The bocage has come from another figure, and the attachment has been skillfully done. Likewise, the figure of Charlotte in figure 202.13 was sold by a very reputable source, and it was described as having a bocage repair. The figure is very much in the style of Enoch Wood, but the bocage is specific to the pot bank referred to in this work as the Tunstall Group. At some point, an enterprising restorer used a bocage from a "Tunstall" figure to restore an Enoch Wood figure. To the knowledgeable, the result is ridiculous.

Figure 202.12. Gardening group. The pinecone bocage is specific to the Patriotic Group, but that pot bank did not make gardening groups of this form. A bocage taken from a Patriotic Group figure has been used to replace the bocage lost from this gardening group.

Figure 202.14. Cribb and Molineux. Despite the size difference, these pairs came from the same molds. Shrinkage of approximately 10% is very visible to the naked eye. *John Howard; www.antiquepottery.co.uk.*

Assess the size. Know that size usually does not matter much. Do not be perturbed if you find a figure just like the one you are evaluating illustrated elsewhere and described as being of a slightly different height. There are gross discrepancies in published figure heights, and it is not uncommon to find that two sources describe the very same figure as differently sized. Human error is to blame. Remember that shrinkage in firing can affect the size of a figure by as much as 10%. The variation is particularly exaggerated to the eye on round objects, such as heads. The two pairs of boxers in figure 202.14 are from the same molds, despite their size difference.

Remember that things happened! Sometimes figures were damaged in manufacture, and they were finished off and sold as is. A performing bear group that was made with the man lacking an arm is shown in this work. Similarly, figures that lost bocage branches or minor components in manufacture do occur, but these are most definitely the exception rather than the rule. Original mistakes like this do not impact value in the same way that damage does. Rather, they convey a quirkiness that is part of the inherent charm of early figures.

Consider the price. If your figure has passed scrutiny, you are now free to fall in love with it. The odds are that it is not perfect—few figures are—but you know that there will be no unpleasant surprises at a later date. What should you pay? An early figure is not a commodity. Each is unique in its own way. It is virtually impossible to find two identical figures in exactly the same condition. Price is largely subjective. If you like the figure and can afford it, buy it. You may wait a life time for another that comes close.

Evaluate the seller. Many sellers are neither as honest nor as knowledgeable as they should be. A lack of both honesty and knowledge is a lethal combination, and it is present to some extent at most levels of the trade. But fortunately, honest and knowledgeable dealers do exist, and they make collecting a pleasure. A good dealer will share everything he or she knows about the figure and will disclose it on your receipt. Insist on a receipt detailing condition. Collecting is fun and rewarding, and charming figures can be bought for a very modest cost. Mistakes, on the other hand, are always expensive. Buyer beware!

203. Addendum

The figures in this chapter are additions to the material recorded in Volumes 1–3 of this work.

Figure 203.1. Lady on horseback, with a dog; with bocage. Probably attributable to Leather Leaf Group. H: 7.7". A companion to figure 31.23 in Volume 2. Price C.

Figure 203.2. Sportsman with dog. H: 8.3". Made without bocage. Price B.

Figure 203.3. Shepherd and shepherdess with dog; with bocage. H: 6.7". These figures occur on separate bases (Vol. 1, figs. 27.100–101). See figure 197.55 from the same pot bank. Price B.

Figure 203.4. Girl reading. Attributed to "Sherratt". H: 6.3". Differs from other "Sherratt" reading maids in Volume 1, chapter 25. Price A.

Figure 203.5. *DR. SYNTAX*. Three figure showing Doctor Syntax landing at Calais, tied to a tree, and playing the violin. H: 6". These are variations of subjects are shown in Volume 2, chapter 36. *John Howard; www.antiquepottery.co.uk.*

Figure 203.6. Lost Sheep Found. H: 8.4". The same model as figure 97.17 in Volume 2 but made without a bocage. Price B. *John Howard; www.antiquepottery.co.uk.*

Figure 203.7. Shepherdess. Attributed to Ralph Wood. H: ~8". Companion model to the shepherd piper in Volume 1, figures 26.206–207. Bocage lost. Price A. *Elinor Penna.*

Figure 203.8. Bull baiting group. Attributed to "Sherratt". L: 15". Thought to be an intermediate model between figures 83.6 and 83.7 in Volume 2. Price E.

Figure 203.9. Dandies. H: 6.2". An unusual petite group made without bocage. See Volume 3, chapter 133 for other dandies. Price B.

Figure 203.10. Bear baiting group. H: 11". See Volume 2, chapter 82 for other groups on this theme. Price D. *John Howard; www.antiquepottery.co.uk*.

Figure 203.11. *SAINT PETER, ST PAUL*. Attributed to Box Title Group. H: 9.5" (L), 9.7"(R). See Volume 2, chapters 104–105 for other examples of these subjects. Price C. *Collection of Eileen and Robert Carde.*

Figure 203.12. Lion. H: 8". An otherwise unrecorded model. See Volume 3, chapter 126 for other lions. Price C. *John Howard; www.antiquepottery.co.uk.*

Figure 203.13. Swan whistle. H: 3.5". See Volume 3, chapter 113 for other bird whistles. Price B. *John Howard; www.antiquepottery.co.uk.*

Index

Italics denote titled figures
The number in **bold font** preceding page numbers indicates the relevant Volume number